226

W9-DJE-684

THE BEATITUDES ARE FOR TODAY

An Exposition of Matthew 5: 1-16

by
GEORGE L. LAWLOR

BAKER BOOK HOUSE
Grand Rapids, Michigan

ISBN: 0-8010-5541-5

Copyright, 1974, by Baker Book House Company

PRINTED IN THE UNITED STATES OF AMERICA

First printing, May 1974
Second printing, December 1974

In
memory of
my wife and my mother, both now with
the Lord. They lived and walked in the truth
of these great pronouncements

PREFACE

There is perhaps no other passage of the Scriptures so deeply spiritual, so fundamentally doctrinal, so correspondingly practical, and therefore so profoundly meaningful, as the great pronouncements of our Lord Jesus Christ entitled "The Beatitudes." These verses in Matthew 5:1-16 set forth, in a manner unsurpassed, *the inner state of mind and heart* which is the indispensable absolute of true Christian discipleship. They also delineate the *outward manifestation of character and conduct* which are the evidence and witness of that genuine discipleship. No true believer can come to this passage and spend time in it—reading, pondering, meditating, laying its truth to heart, desiring its blessedness to be established not only within, but also outwardly in daily life—*and come away the same.*

The Greek texts of Nestle, Souter, and Westcott and Hort, and the Hebrew Old Testament text of Rudolph Kittel have been used in the exposition. Reference has also been made to the Septuagint Version of the Old Testament and to parts of the photographic facsimile edition of the Codex Alexandrinus of the New Testament. For the English reading, the King James Version in the new Scofield edition of 1967 has been used throughout.

CONTENTS

Part Three

INTRODUCTION

The Sermon on the Mount has long been a center of controversy. Modernism teaches that salvation depends upon keeping this sermon, and makes it the sum and substance of the Gospel. It is regarded by others as Law, and not as Gospel, and Jesus is said to be here expounding the true sense of the Law over against the distorted expositions and interpretations of the Jewish scribes and rabbis. There are some who consider it to be a constitution intended only for the subjects of the Kingdom during the Millennial Age, and which cannot be applied to Christians today. Still others recognize the spiritual truth in the Sermon on the Mount, but hold its high precepts to be impossible of attainment in the present age. We do not deliberately seek argument over this great passage of Holy Scripture, but we must strongly advocate its application to the true church today. Believers should not be deprived of its blessedness, for it is profitable for doctrine, reproof, correction, and instruction in righteousness in our day, and its truth is particularly important and relevant for the days in which we live.

We do not find basic, fundamental Law here, for Law cannot produce the state of blessedness set forth in the first part of Matthew 5. Still, it is true that, as Rudolph Stier wrote, "It deepens into a spiritual and strict interpretation of the letter of the Law, and requires on the ground of the promised grace the righteousness of God for the kingdom of God."[1] This section is basic and necessary to all that follows in Matthew 5, 6, 7, for

---

[1]*Words of the Lord Jesus* (Philadelphia: Smith, English and Company, 1859), p. 94.

Christ characterizes His hearers in 5:1-16 as true disciples, and the entire discourse is addressed to them. Contrast is drawn between Law and Gospel by the Lord Himself: "Ye have heard that it has been said . . . but I say unto you. . . ." The connective "but" is de, not alla, for the milder note of contrast is in keeping with the fact that the Law has its place in the divine economy and is fulfilled in the Lord Jesus Christ. This manner of speech appears seven times in the body of Matthew 5. *Seven* is the number of Holy Scripture for divine perfection found in our Lord Jesus Christ, and the Law is the pedagogue which brings us to Him (Gal. 3:23-25).

The body of the Sermon on the Mount deals with the life of Christ's true disciples, and concerns Law only as a rule by which these disciples are to conduct themselves and show that they are true disciples. While the extended passage does indeed present the divine constitution for the government of our Lord Jesus Christ over the earth during the coming Kingdom period, it certainly is not without meaning and significance for His true disciples today. Here we have the framework and structure for the new life and experience entered by means of regeneration. It gives the outline, or model, of the new life of the saved, the shape into which it is to be molded. To those who prate over salvation resting in "living the Sermon on the Mount," we say simply that the cross is required to transform each of the grand precepts in this great discourse into living experience.

Stier's comment on the arrangement of the Sermon is splendid and very much to the point:

> We have absolute and special promise, as the origin and foundation of all, in the Benedictions (v. 3-12); then on the ground of their assurance (ye are! ye have!) the evidence and manifestation of that new life and light is demanded (vs. 13-16); finally, there is here also a warning, which in its emphatic restriction and rejection, points forward already to the test at the end of all (vs. 17-20). Even this last rigorous test indeed is still under the high note of promise:—I am come to fulfill![2]

---

[2]Op. cit., p. 96.

F. B. Meyer calls the Sermon on the Mount "The Directory of the Devout Life," the key to which is found in Matthew 5:1-16. Lenski remarks that it speaks of "the works of Christ's true disciples, which they are to do in the power of the faith." We agree with the words of these great expositors and accept the passage as one which sets forth the state of believers now, an index to the spiritual state in which they are to abide, and a description of the spiritual life they are to live. Christians are surely meant to drink deeply of the truth in these verses and to realize the Sermon's exquisite ideals. They are the "good works" of Matthew 5:16, the evidences of character, qualities of godliness and holiness which testify to the presence of Christ within.[3] They are those marks of true discipleship which our Lord Jesus Christ desires to see in His own, those for which He alone is sufficient.

---

[3]Every one of these Beatitudes may be found in essence, if not in exact terminology, in the two great lists of Christian fruits and virtues, as set forth by Paul in Galatians 5:22-23, and by Peter in II Peter 1:5-7. See these passages.

Part One

THE PEOPLE FOR WHOM
THE BEATITUDES ARE INTENDED

(vv. 1-2)

1

THE SERMON IS DIRECTED TO THOSE WHO ARE THE DISCIPLES OF CHRIST

(vv. 1-2)

Christ's disciples came to Him. *"And when He sat down, His disciples came to Him"* (v. 1).

All attention is to be centered on the Lord's teaching. This is clear, for the circumstances are simple and the preliminaries are brief. From Luke's record (Luke 6:12 ff.), we learn that the Lord went up into a mountain to pray and continued in prayer all that night. Then in the morning He chose the Twelve as apostles, came part way down the mountain with them, and selected a spot on the mountainside where all could see and hear Him, and began His teaching. Many make much of the expression "the mountain," and stress the article with the noun, to oros, as reaching back to Mt. Sinai and the giving of the Law. The mountain in Matthew 5 is thus conceived to be "the New Testament Sinai," reminding us that as the Saviour of the New Covenant, who is Himself the fulfillment of the Law, teaches the blessedness of those who have been saved by grace—so we are to think of the sacred mountain of Old Testament history from which issued forth the Lord's Commandments of condemnation. As we consider Matthew's record of the Beatitudes and observe the presence of the Lord in the mountain, it is perhaps somewhat natural that we should remember Mt. Sinai, "the mountain of the Law." However the definite article with the noun is better taken to point out particularly what the Lord's teaching made of that mountain, i.e., the singular and definite importance of the mountain because of the remarkable verities set forth there that morning by the Lord. This is the significance we should see in "the mountain" (to oros). It is not the mountain in itself that is so meaningful, but rather the profound body of truth taught from one of its plateaus.

After the Lord sat down (kathisantos autou), His disciples came to Him. "His disciples" (hoi matheitai autou) include the twelve apostles chosen by the Lord prior to the teaching (cf. Luke 6:12 ff.), and other disciples as well. While matheitai is applied particularly in certain passages to the Twelve (cf. Matt. 10:1; John 2:2), the word includes all who believe the message of Christ and receive Him as Saviour and Messiah (cf. John 19:38; Acts 6:1). True believers in all generations are "disciples" (matheitai) of the Lord Jesus Christ. The message of the Sermon is for those who have been saved by grace, who are recipients of the implanted Word. Those disciples who were there that day on the mountainside with the Lord were the immediate recipients of these blessed truths. But they were spoken by Christ and recorded by Matthew for those who become disciples of the Lord in any and every age. The word *disciples* means somewhat more than merely "learners, beginners." One may be a Christian of considerable learning and experience and be called a "disciple." It may also refer to those who have learned much and are still learning.

When the Lord was seated, "His disciples came unto him." The verb proseilthan describes the fact of the disciples' coming to their Master. The aorist tense denotes their approach as being definite and purposive. They came down the mountain with the Lord to the place which He chose to begin His teaching, and there they gathered around Him expectantly, for the purpose of learning, imbibing more of His words. There they received the instruction which follows in the record of Matthew. With such an attitude, we—His disciples today—must also come to Him and gather about Him. Let us come to Him daily, expectantly, with definite purpose and intention. We come to learn from Him (Matt. 11:29), by His Spirit, in the Word. We receive instruction in this manner, and we must seek the Lord with hearts that are willing to be taught, ready to receive the truth and obey it. Amid the extraordinary pressures, tensions, and frustrations of our time, it is Christ alone who has the proper words for our hearts, and it is the Lord alone whose message is all-sufficient for the troubled minds of those who are seeking answers for pressing the perplexing problems. In all the universe there is no one else in whom there is rest for the weary soul and life for the perishing sinner. Peter said: "Lord, to whom shall we go? *Thou* hast the words of eternal life" (John 6:68). It is to *Him* that men and women of our day, as in Peter's day, may come definitely and expectantly, for the purpose of hearing— not what they may *want* to hear, but what they *need* to hear, without becoming victims of deception and seduction, and not being turned away in a state of confused desperation.

Christ taught His disciples. *"And he opened his mouth and taught them, saying . . ."* (v. 2).

Luke 6:20 adds to Matthew's account the significant fact that the Lord "lifted up (eparas) his eyes on his disciples." By merging the two accounts at this point, the sense would be: "Having lifted up His eyes unto His disciples, and having opened His mouth, He began to teach them. . . ." Luke's mention of this preliminary action by the Lord is not ambiguous. There is a bit of teaching in this very action for us—insignificant as it may seem to be. The Lord lifted up His eyes (the aorist participle eparas denotes definite and particular action; it is not merely incidental) to His disciples, beholding those who were immediately around Him, fixing upon His true disciples and seeing in them the type and earnest of all those future disciples whom He would call out of the multitudes of unbelievers and self-styled followers of Christ down through the centuries. Then He directed to His disciples, (Luke 6:20, eis tous matheitas autou) the teaching concerning the *kind* of men they must be whom He calls out and receives, and by His further teaching and direction prepares for Himself and His work. Hence, first of all there is the truth of *the internal state of mind and heart* which is the result of the regenerative call of God, i.e., the salvation that grace provides and which is therefore the indispensable basis for all true discipleship. Inasmuch then, as those who through regeneration by the Holy Spirit, with the instrumentality of the Word, become genuine disciples of the Lord, are declared righteous and invested with a righteousness placed by God to their account, so *the outward conduct and deportment* follow—which is required as the witness and proof of true discipleship. In this manner the Lord taught His disciples, and thus must all who are true believers *expect* to be taught.

The verb "taught" is the Greek edidasken, the ingressive imperfect form of didasko, "to impart instruction, indoctrinate, explain and expound." The ingressive imperfect describes the action of Christ as He began to teach, and was continuing that teaching. It is an invitation to follow that teaching, a gentle but perpetual pressure to hearken to it and obey. The words that flowed from His mouth were supernatural words, for He is a supernatural Person; they were solemn, impressive, binding words which brought the power and authority of God before the minds of men. But they were gracious words too, and remind us of Luke 4:22, where Luke tells us that when the Lord read the words of Scripture in the synagogue, the people "all bore him witness, and wondered at the *gracious* words which proceeded out of his mouth. . . ."

Matthew goes on to tell us that the Lord began to teach "them" (autous), the accusative plural pronoun referring to the disciples (hoi matheitai). The Lord Jesus Christ began to instruct *them,* and continued doing so. *They,* His own disciples, received His teaching. The multitudes who may have heard were secondary. This teaching was for those who believed in Him and continued to believe in Him (John 8:31, "Then said Jesus to those Jews who believed on him, If ye continue in my word, then are ye my disciples indeed"), and is directed to those who know Him redemptively today, or in any day. Others may hear, and do hear, but remain obstinate in their unbelief. They must hear and believe, and continue to believe. How can those who do not believe comprehend such extraordinary teaching:

"Blessed are the poor in spirit . . . they that mourn . . . the meek . . .?" Such teaching is contrary to all humanistic concepts of rightness with God and the way men want to walk in this modern age. These are days of growing might and prowess, strife for superiority of one force or power over another, of human accomplishment by almost any means regardless of cost to others. Today the end justifies the means, whatever they may be. Our age is not one in which the poor, the mourners, the meek ones, the pure in heart, the peacemakers find themselves particularly favored. That the Lord should pronounce as "blessed" such people as this is astonishing, in view of the fact that the world does precisely the opposite. Nevertheless as Christ was teaching *then,* so He is teaching *now,* through His faithful servants, His true disciples, who are in the world for the express purpose of heralding the truth. As they speak to the Lord's people words of edification, instruction, inspiration, and sanctification, others may hear, but only secondarily. This great passage is for the saved; it is not a Gospel tract for the unsaved. It is intended for the people of God, those who are His by redemption as well as by creation. The Sermon on the Mount places before them the deeply spiritual characteristics of the devout and godly life, that life and daily walk which God expects of every true believer.

2

THE SUBJECTS OF THE DISCOURSE ARE CHARACTERIZED BY THE WORD *BLESSED*

(vv. 3-11)

The Greek word for "blessed" is the adjective makarios. It appears in the nominative plural form nine times in this passage. Nine verses begin with it. The word and its cognates occur fifty times in the New Testament. It is an exceptional word, purposefully used in an exceptional manner to convey an exceptional message. Let us consider it as it is used by the One who came to give the "blessedness" of which He spoke.

The word describes a condition of the soul.

Makarioi is similar to the poetic makar, literally "happy, blissful, blessed." In five of the passages where it occurs, it is rendered "happy," and in the others is translated "blessed," at once recalling the Hebrew ashera in Psalm 1:1, *"Blessed* is the man. . . ."* Homer used the word to describe a wealthy man, and Herodotus used it in writing of an oasis in the desert. It is also used by Plato as descriptive of one who is prosperous. Both Homer and Hesiod spoke of the Greek gods as being "blessed" in themselves, unaffected by the world of men who are subject to poverty, weakness, and death. From this usage it appears that the word seems to have designated an inner state or condition of being which is neither the result of external circumstances nor subject to change produced by outside forces. Such is the basic connotation of the term in its use in the New Testament.

The word thus describes that state of happiness and bliss, well-being and blessedness, in which all true believers stand. It denotes that blest condition of soul possessed by those whose sins are forgiven, from whose consciences the burden of guilt has been removed, and who have thus been reconciled to God. "Blessed" (makarios) is the state of that person whose heart is indwelt by the Lord Himself, and who thus is walking with Him (see Ps. 32:1-2; 40:1-4; 65:4; 119:1-2; 128:1; Rom. 4:6-8; Gal. 3:9; Rev. 14:13; 19:9; 20:6). The word standing first in each sentence down to verse 11, has neither eisin ("are") or esontal ("shall be") used with it, although the present "are" has been inserted in the text of the Authorized Version, and correctly— "Blessed *are*. . . ." It is a simple statement, but contains the whole fullness of all that God's plenteous mercy offers for the acceptance of faith. It involves and embraces not only the idea that we *are now* and immediately blessed, but also that we *shall be* blessed ever more and more as time moves on toward the day of perfection with the Lord of glory.

Thus it is a state or condition which may be entered and enjoyed here and now, not one to be postponed until we enter our heavenly home. The blessedness does not come as a reward for merit, nor it is given in recompense for a long life of noble deeds, neither is it obtained after long service in halls of learning or fields of religious endeavor. It does not consist in material possessions, abundance of worldly goods, or in social prestige. It is realized simply and only by coming in humble faith to the One who taught it to His disciples of that day, and by whose power and grace it has been preserved for His disciples of this day. "Come unto me, all ye . . . and learn from me."

The word is indicative of character.

The most striking thing about makarios is the fact that it is used to describe the very nature and character of God and of our Lord Jesus Christ. The Septuagint Version has the word in Psalm 68:35, *"Blessed* [be] God"; in Psalm 72:18, *"Blessed* [be] the Lord God . . . "; and in Psalm 119:12, *"Blessed* [art]

Thou, O Lord. . . ." These statements are clearly descriptive of the absolutely holy and righteous nature of God, with all that is eternally and infinitely woven into His character and not acquired in any sense. In I Timothy 1:11, the apostle Paul writes: "According to the glorious gospel of the *blessed* God. . . ." This inspired record leaves no doubt as to the mind of Paul with regard to the exalted nature of the God who had called him, enabled him, counted him faithful, and put him into the ministry. Again, in I Timothy 6:15, the apostle uses the term makarios, this time of the Lord Jesus Christ particularly. He refers to Him as "the *blessed* and only Potentate, the King of kings, and Lord of lords." This remarkable description that includes the word *blessed* makes clear that Paul was being very careful to mark out the high and holy, unique and princely character of the eternal Son of God.

Since this word is used as a special designation of the nature and character of God and of our Lord Jesus Christ, and in view of the fact that II Peter 1:4 clearly states that believers are made "partakers of the divine nature," the application of the word makarioi to the subjects of the Beatitudes is unquestionably indicative of *character*. This teaching is for those who bear the character of regenerated ones, true believers in Christ, and cannot be indiscriminately applied to all churchmembers or people at large who are swept up in various religious movements. It must be clearly understood by all that the blessedness set forth by the word makarios is fundamentally a definite quality of God's own character, and cannot be claimed apart from Him. No man can be the recipient of the blessedness of Matthew 5:1-16, if he is not a partaker of the divine nature of the Son of God. One must call upon the name of the Lord, confess Him as God and Saviour, believe in the heart that He has been raised from the dead, and then this blessedness will become a reality in the life, and will endure forever.

It is obvious then, from these considerations of the word makarioi, that the people for whom the teaching of this great discourse is intended are Christian believers, born-again ones, true disciples of the Lord Jesus Christ, in every age since the

Sermon was delivered. Identification with Christ at the cross is necessary to transform each of these grand precepts into a living, gracious, blessed experience. With the possession of the new life, of which the resurrection is the guarantee, there comes the molding and development of the outline, or model, set forth in this great discourse. What a truly blessed directory of the spiritual life this passage is! It should be studied carefully, intensely, and meditatively by the saved. It should be laid deeply to heart, with a constraining desire for a more profound and abiding knowledge and experience of the devout life. If you will set your mind to these sublime truths and meditate over them with earnestness and honesty of heart, you cannot come away the same.

3

THE SENSE OF THE PASSAGE
IS ENTIRELY AND DEEPLY SPIRITUAL

This has already been made clear, but there are certain other considerations which must be singled out for careful observation:

1. Note that there is not one reference to the social and political aspects of the Kingdom, those perspectives in which the Jews were so vitally interested.

2. Note that there is peculiar stress laid upon *being,* and not upon doing, ruling, possessing. The verb "are" is in italics except in verses 11, 13, 14. But the sense of the passage permits it in each case. It is what a man *is* that counts most.

3. Note that the terms used to describe the subjects of this passage and the elements of their blessedness are directly contrary to all the human ideas of kingdoms and governments. Prevalence of power and the premise that men are good form the basis for the building of peace and prosperity, according to human philosophy. This, of course, is wrong—as is evidenced here in the Beatitudes.

4. Note that while the position of those described as blessed is the most exalted and influential in the godly sense, it is the basest from the standpoint of the world.

5. Note that persecution is set forth here as a requisite for the blessed ones, and no authority for retaliation appears. This is the process through which we must pass in the character of the godly (see II Tim. 3:12).

6. Note the change of person from "they" in verses 3-10, to "ye" (plural) in verses 11-18. This leaves no doubt as to how the disciples are to apply these beatitudes to themselves—even

though they are spoken in the third person in the first part of the teaching. Moreover, the abrupt change to the second person, while it is not expressed by the emphatic pronoun, makes its impression upon *us*—as it is intended to do—and causes *us* to be aware of the force of individual, personal application. The spiritual character of this teaching and its personal claim on *us* is thus driven home to *our* hearts and minds, although we are far removed from the time and place of its speaking.

7. Note the twofold expression of purpose in this passage, which sums up the reasons for the living of such a life: " . . . for my sake" (eneken emou, v. 11); " . . . and glorify your Father which is in heaven" (kai doxasosen ton patera humon ton en tois ouranois, v. 16).

This is spiritual. Each of the pronouncements looks ahead to this double expression of purpose and finds herein its anchor and its base.

Part Two

THE PRONOUNCEMENTS
OF SPIRITUAL BLESSEDNESS

(vv. 3-12)

In the Beatitudes we find set forth the elements which comprise the experience of the devout life. They are the ingredients, the marks of discipleship, the ideals of character, as our Lord taught them. They are the qualities of blessedness which marked *His* life, and He desires that they be repeated in *us*. They may be apprehended, but only as we give room to Him, only as He fills us with Himself. As the vine abides in the branches, and the branches in the vine, these fruits are possible, but "without me, ye can do nothing" (John 15:5b).

Each of these pronouncements has two elements: (1) the aspect of blessedness, and (2) the assurance in which the blessedness consists.

The first four pronouncements look toward God, while the last five look somewhat more to men.

1

THE FIRST PRONOUNCEMENT

"Blessed [are] the poor in spirit;
for theirs is the kingdom of heaven."

(v. 3)

The Aspect of Blessedness

"Blessed [are] the poor in spirit. . . ."

makarioi hoi ptochoi to pneumati

The Condition of Poverty

The word ptochos is derived from the verb ptosso, which denotes *a shrinking from something, or somebody; to cower and cringe like a beggar.* In classical Greek, it describes one who is reduced to beggary, who slinks about and crouches here and there begging, asking alms, often it involves the act of roving about in wretchedness. Both ptochos ("beggar") and ptochei ("beggar-woman") occur frequently in the early Greek writings.[1] This classical use is illustrated in the New Testament in such passages as Luke 14:13, "When thou givest a feast, call the *poor* [ptochous]. . . ." or Luke 16:20, "And there was a certain beggar [ptochos]. . . ."

The word is used further in the New Testament in a sense not

---

[1] See ptochos, Hom. Od. 14.400, 18:1, 21'327, etc. Hdt. 3:14, Ar. Pl.552, E. Med. 515. ptochei, Ath. 10:453a, S.CC 444. Henry George Liddell and Robert Scott, *A Greek-English Lexicon* (New York: Harper & Bros., Publishers, 1870), p.1300.

quite so strict, to describe those who are poor and needy as contrasted to hol plouslol the wealthy, those who abound in material resources; (cf. Matt. 19:21; John 12:5, 8; Rom. 15:26; Gal. 2:10; James 2:2, 3, 6). It is also frequently used in a still broader sense of those who possess no wealth, influence, position, and honor, i.e., lowly and afflicted, as in Matthew 11:5, "the *poor* [ptochol] have the gospel preached to them...." Furthermore, the word occurs in Revelation 3:17, where it marks apostates who are destitute of the Christian virtues and the riches of eternal life: "Because thou sayest, I am rich, and increased with goods, and have need of nothing, and knowest not that thou art wretched, and miserable, and *poor* [ptochos]...." It is the word used in II Corinthians 8:9 to describe the poverty of our Lord's descent into the realm of the flesh for the purpose of substitutionary atonement for sins: hoti di' humas eptocheusen plousios on hina humeis tei ekeinou ptocheia plouteiseite, ("that though he was rich, yet for your sakes He became *poor,* that ye through His *poverty* might be rich"). It is a stronger word, for example, than peneis, "poor," which is used in II Corinthians 9:9, "He hath given to the *poor*...." The man described by peneis is poor to the extent that he must earn his own livelihood by daily labor. But ptochos is the individual who is so poor that he must obtain his living by begging. He has to depend upon other peoples' alms. His help must come from outside sources, he is an object of charity. There are some people today who are like the ptochos, who cannot help themselves, who are in need of charity, and should be given succor by those who are able.

It may occur to someone to ask: Why did the Holy Spirit of God select *this word* for the text? Why did the Lord use *this word* when He spoke back there so long ago and made His first pronouncement? We might suggest that it was because the word so aptly describes the native conditions of man—helpless, poverty-stricken, hopeless, needing God. Spiros Zodhiates remarks:

It was to convey His diagnosis of man. He is empty, poor, helpless, he cannot work for his own salvation. He is ptochos, not peneis. He needs mercy from outside himself. And this is the condition of fallen man. No one from his own level, his household environment, can help him. His help must come from someone who is superior, from above, from God.[2]

We are totally dependent upon the grace and mercy of the eternal God. We are empty and helpless, and cannot help ourselves. But Christ fills that emptiness with Himself and His words, supplying the help and hope that are certain and everlasting. Through Him and because of what He has done, we become full of His salvation and of the grace and mercy of the Lord. Yet a paradox remains: to be filled with Christ and the hope of glory which His presence brings, is to be empty of self and the pride of the human spirit.

Hence the word may be rendered as "one who is beggarly poor," and the articular plural substantive hoi ptochoi as "the beggarly poor ones." This is the term which has been taken by the Holy Spirit and ennobled in certain New Testament passages, where inspiration has given it a special and particular significance. It is likewise the word used in the text (Matt. 5:3), to set forth the condition of those who are declared by Christ as *blessed*. It is astonishing that our Lord should pronounce people such as this *blessed,* i.e., happy, fortunate, blissful, rich, in the highest degree. Religionists, social-reformers, philosophers, and people of the world would generally do the very opposite. For ordinarily people are not congratulated and blessed because they are poor, or have afflictions. The present philosophy of life desires to see all poverty and pain eliminated. But those are *blessed* who, having been brought into the family of God as His own true children, now realize their complete emptiness without Him and confess this need for total reliance and dependence upon Him, knowing that without Him they are nothing. With Him, and by His enablement, we find it possible to face whatever is ahead of us, the poverty and the pain, the difficult and the dangerous, without over-anxiety and without fear.

---

[2]*Poverty, a Blessing or a Curse?* (New York: American Board of Missions to Greeks, Inc., Publishers, 1962), p. 27.

This cannot refer to a state of temporal, material beggarliness in which the saved are pronounced *blessed.* Of course, we can be beggarly poor in the physical sense and still be blessed. But poverty does not produce blessedness, nor is it a necessary condition for becoming blessed. Neither does it mean that we are poor simply because we are blessed. On the other hand it is also true that godly men are not always materially poor. Nicodemus and Joseph of Arimathea were materially wealthy, as apparently were Philemon and the centurion of Luke 8:1-10. Such are few in number, however, as compared to believers who are not wealthy in material things. Paul states: "Not many wise men after the flesh, not many mighty, not many noble, are called" (I Cor. 1:26). Notwithstanding, the state described by ptochos is not indicative of temporal, physical beggarliness, for the Scriptures declare that the needs of the saved shall be supplied. David testifies that in all his years he never saw the righteous forsaken, nor his seed begging bread (Ps. 37:25). In the account of Paul concerning his hardships and sufferings as a servant of Jesus Christ (cf. I Cor. 4:9-13; II Cor. 6:1-10; 11:23-28), there is mention of hunger and thirst, but no reference to a cringing poverty, no allusion to his being forced to beg bread. While the earthly life of our Lord may properly be described as "poor," while His descent from the wealth and glory of heaven was by comparison into the realm of poverty, and while His self-humbling took Him to the extremity of humiliation—yet at no time did He appear as a beggarly poor one in the sight of men. Wherever He went, He commanded the respect and attention of others. Neither, equally true, did His apostles appear as beggarly poor ones in the sight of men. They were called "unlearned and ignorant," accused of "turning the world upside down," and of being "mad," and it is probable that they were the objects of many other accusations and epithets. But never do we read or hear of them as "beggarly poor"—destitute and without help, cringing at someone's door-step, begging food.

The definite article hoi particularizes these poor ones. They are not beggars in general, but a specific group; not common, ordinary beggars, but particular ones standing out from all others. These are beggars who have been pronounced *blessed* by the Lord of glory, beggars who possess the character of blessed ones, beggars whose beggarliness is identified by the words which follow. We must be poor and humble *in spirit* if this divine blessedness is to abide in our hearts.

The Connection with Spirit

The articular dative explains the beggarliness expressed by hoi ptochoi. We regard the dative as that of *reference,* or *relation* ("connection with")—beggarly poor ones *with relation to,* i.e., in connection with, the spirit.[3] The article with the dative noun emphasizes and particularizes this relation. It is in connection with the spirit, and not with an external realm, that the beggarly poor character subsists. It is the beggarliness with respect to the spirit, the inner man, that is set forth here—not a poverty in connection with goods and assets, not a poverty of insufficient food, clothing, and other necessities of life. It is that spirit which bows to such a poverty in deep submission rather than to rebel against it, which is so often true of one who faces temporal poverty. It is such as that set forth in Isaiah 66:2, "but to this man will I look, even to him that is poor and of a contrite spirit, and trembleth at my word."

Blessedness is thus pronounced upon those who are beggarly poor with relation to the spirit. Here is the first ideal of character, the first mark of true discipleship, the first ingredient of the devout life taught by this passage: "beggarly poor in connection with the spirit." By nature and disposition we are not inclined to be beggarly poor in the spirit, but rather to the contrary—proud and selfish. Conquest over the old self lies only in the transforming power of the indwelling Holy Spirit who leads us to all truth in the Word. Here we learn of Him who loved us and gave Himself for us—and if this does not bring

---

[3]See Rom. 6:2; 8:12; I Cor. 6:12; II Cor. 5:13, for this dative construction.

change into our lives there is nothing that will. He Himself has left us the example supreme: "Let this mind be in *you,* which was also in Christ Jesus, who being in the form of God, thought it not robbery to be equal with God, but emptied himself . . . and humbled himself. . . ."

This is the mind that must be in us. This reveals the poverty with respect to the spirit which must mark our daily life. We come to see that we are nothing without Him, to confess that He is all. We are led to the place where we are willing to lean our whole weight on Him, not to insist on our own way, not to demand our own rights, not to persist in following our own schemes and plans, not to erect our own edifice, not to grasp all that is ours with a stubborn refusal to sacrifice for others, not to be so insistent upon the amount of profit and gain for ourselves—but to learn that we have no power of our own, that we are useful and profitable only as we submit to Christ, and become channels through which He may pour out His grace, love, and power. God says, "Pride, and arrogance, and the evil way, and the perverse mouth, do I hate" (Prov. 8:13), but the other side of the matter is to "humble yourselves in the sight of the Lord and he shall lift you up" (James 4:10). As Lenski comments, "These wretched beggars bring absolutely nothing to God but their complete emptiness and need, and stoop in the dust for pure grace and mercy only."[4]

The Assurance in Which the Blessedness Consists

" . . . because theirs is the kingdom of the heavens."

hoti auton estin hei basileia ton ouranon

The Position of the Pronoun Is Emphatic

The plural pronoun auton, "theirs," is forward in the sentence, which gives it a particular emphasis: "*Theirs* is the king-

---

[4]*The Interpretation of St. Matthew's Gospel* (Columbus, Ohio: Wartburg Press, 1943) p. 184.

dom. . . ." This is the assurance of possession: *theirs* in the sense of *theirs alone,* barring all others who are not of the makarioi, who approach God with a different spirit than that of beggarliness.

Theirs equals *ours.* And *ours* may be broken down to the individual *mine,* so that each of these beggarly poor ones—each of *us*—may say over and over again, "*Mine* is the kingdom of the heavens." We have done nothing to earn this, nothing to deserve it, yet it is *ours.* We may talk about *our* this and that, *my* this and that, but there is nothing to equal *this,* and there is no greater comfort and assurance than in *this.* Let us lay it to heart. We—the beggars in connection with the spirit by the grace of God—have the Kingdom. It is *ours.* To all who stoop before God with the empty hearts and empty hands of beggars, He has given the Kingdom. We have it, but let us remember that we have it only gift-wise. It has come to us out of God's eternal heart of love and grace. He has made us meet to be partakers of it, and He has translated us into it only upon the basis of redemption through the blood of His Son.

The Present Tense of the Verb Is Significant

The present estin, from eimi, marks present, continuing reality. Surely this answers the interpreters who state that only a future possession of the Kingdom is indicated here because the verses which follow have future tenses. But they seem to forget, or overlook verses 10-11, where present tenses again occur. The text reads estin (*is, is now*). This is assurance in the present. The Kingdom is theirs (ours) *now.* Let us think of it in that way. It is possible for each of us to live momentarily in the reality, in the positive assurance, that the Kingdom *is* ours. It was ours at eight o'clock this morning, and at nine, and ten; it is still ours at noon; and will be ours at midnight tonight. There is *no time* when the Kingdom is not ours.

Then there must be no time during our waking hours, when we live, i.e., eat, drink, think, speak, move, and walk about, conduct ourselves in all ways, other than that in which we are aware that we possess the Kingdom, that we are beggars in the spirit who are the objects of God's grace.

The Possession Is the Kingdom

The grand concept "the kingdom of the heavens," hei basileia ton ouranon, is not to be compared with earthly kingdoms as we know them and the conditions which exist in them. "The kingdom of the heavens" cannot be taken in the sense of a mere external realm. It is the same Kingdom as that of 3:2 and 4:17, and thus involves the Messianic rule of our Lord Jesus Christ. It has an earthly aspect, for the remnant of Israel will be returned to her land, redeemed, and restored in accord with the promises and prophecies, and will be the center of the Millennial Kingdom, while certain nations designated as "sheep" (Matthew 25:31-33), will be ushered into the Kingdom as earthly inhabitants—redeemed subjects. But there is something more than this, above and beyond the mere earthly, to be found here.

It is to be observed that the "blessed ones" of 5:1-12, are not addressed as *subjects* of the Kingdom, but rather as *partakers in its rule*. "Theirs *is* the kingdom. . . ." They are *possessors in it* rather than *subjects of it*. Theirs is the Kingdom in that they are partakers of the King's rule and kingship, possessors of royalty and dominion with the King in His Kingdom. In this blessed, presently invisible Kingdom, which is already in the world in the sense that wherever the King is, in His grace and power, there too is the Kingdom—we already bear the title "kings unto God," literally "a kingdom, priests to God" (Rev. 1:6; 5:10). This involves the very regality of the throne of the King, for He Himself has said, "To him that overcometh will I grant to sit with me in my throne" (Rev. 3:21). It is said of the saved that they shall appear with Christ in glory (Col. 3:4); that they shall judge the world and the angels (I Cor. 6:2, 3); that if they suffer they shall reign with Christ (II Tim. 2:12); that they shall reign with Christ in the Millennial Kingdom (Rev. 20:6); and that they shall reign forever and ever (Rev. 22:5). Our kingship with Christ in His throne is wondrously set forth in His marriage to His espoused wife (Rev. 19:7-9), that blessed, indescribable, spiritual union which takes place in heaven, just prior to the King's return in glory, to reign over the earth with His church (Rev. 19:11-16; 5:10). This magnificently illustrates the blessed and unspeakable intimacy of "Theirs is the kingdom. . . ."

Thus the kingdom of the heavens is *ours.* The world would not agree with this concept, for such a kingdom is completely foreign to the world's system. Earthly kingdoms do not have beggars as their kings; they do not look to the poor in spirit as their royalty. Earthly kingdoms, which are many and various, make their kings and unmake them. Today kings may rule, and tomorrow they may be deposed, but those in the Kingdom of Heaven already have their royal titles, already have their Kingdom, although the actual exercise of royalty awaits their crowning, and they will never be deposed. The Kingdom of Christ is a Kingdom of grace and glory. The grace is now unmistakably evident, operative, and blessed indeed (I John 3:1-2a), but the glory has not yet been revealed (I John 3:2b).

May we add that perhaps the greatest evidence, the most blessed assurance that the Kingdom of Heaven *is* ours, is the fact that while we bear the designation of royalty, yet as long as we live in this world of sin and evil, we must cry out to the King for help, and our beggars' hands must be stretched out to Him. *And He keeps us abundantly full,* full of grace, mercy, and strength. He *keeps* His royal ones. Whatever is ahead in the Kingdom, He *now,* in the present, provides for us a vast abundance of riches. He is ever faithful to us and makes us unutterably glad that we are kings. From election to glorification, we march on in triumphant procession, not viewed as royalty here and now, yet knowing that we are even now corulers with Christ. Poor in spirit we are, but rich toward God, carrying with us the wealth of all spiritual blessings in heavenly places in Christ, to that place of divine appointment which awaits our presence with Him who loved us and gave Himself for us. Thus the Kingdom is *ours now* and, being ours, "in its progress it will bring us all that God still has laid up for us."[5]

---

[5]Lenski, op. cit., p. 186.

2

THE SECOND PRONOUNCEMENT

"Blessed [are] they that mourn;
for they shall be comforted."

(v. 4)

The Aspect of Blessedness

"Blessed [are] they that mourn. . . ."

makarioi hoi penthountes

The Sense in Which the Mourning Is to Be Taken

The expression "those [the ones] who are mourning" (hoi penthountes) is a present participle with the plural article, and is rendered properly "the mourning ones," or "the ones who are mourning." The verb itself (pentheo) means "to mourn, lament for the dead, grieve over a severe and painful loss." While it is the most intensive term in Greek to express *mourning,* it describes a more or less self-contained grief which manifests itself externally but does not become excessively violent in its manifestation.[6] The word is most fitting in this text because of its

---

[6]There are nine Greek verbs expressing grief in some aspect, which appear in the New Testament. See the following:
alaladzo: "wail in oriental style"
dakruo: "shed tears"
threineo: "grieve formally"
klaio: "cry audibly as a child"
koptomai: "smite the breast in anguish"
lupeo: "grieve deeply"

self-restraint. It most appropriately sets forth the mourning of the believer, which is mourning on account of the inner ground and first cause of all sorrow and misery—*sin*. Hence, a logical sequence in the Beatitudes should be noted here. The lowly in heart will be sensitive to sin and will be quick to mourn over it. But their mourning is not at all like the mourning of the world, which makes itself heard in its hopelessness, and howls loud enough when its sins find it out.

No one can deny that there is a great deal of sorrow and mourning of one kind or another in the world today. All of us have seen it, have been made aware of it, and have somehow been affected by it. We grieve over disaster and catastrophe, and the awful calamities which result in grim tragedy and dreadful loss of life. Certainly we mourn over famine, earthquake, and war, and the suffering and sorrow they bring. We mourn over pestilence and disease and the death they cause, and we are shocked at the evil and corruption which ruin so many lives and take such a monstrous toll. As the mounting tide of apostasy increases and advances, and as the age nears its predicted end, we may expect the conditions of sorrow and mourning to intensify. Our Lord Jesus Christ spoke particularly of this, when He said, as recorded in Matthew 24:4-8:

> And Jesus answered and said unto them, Take heed that no man deceive you. For many shall come in my name, saying, I am Christ; and shall deceive many. And ye shall hear of wars and rumors of wars; see that ye be not troubled; for all these things must come to pass, but the end is not yet. For nation shall rise against nation, and kingdom against kingdom; and there shall be famines and pestilences, and earthquakes, in various places. All these are the beginning of sorrows.

Those who belong to Christ must feel keenly the terror and evil of sin, and surely must shudder and weep at the sight of its

---

oduromai: lament audibly"
pentheo: "mourn intensely"
stenadzo: "express grief by making sounds and groanings"

awful work in the world. But as we turn from the sin in the world, from beholding the woes, wrongs, injustices, the anguish, pain, oppression, and wickedness so rampant everywhere, to our own sins—the tears must flow even more freely. For we must realize then, the awful power of sin, its effects in us, and our own helplessness against it. Hence this mourning is a great cry to God of repentance and contrition, and of confession in our distress, and a plea for mercy and grace. It is sorrow because of *sin itself,* not merely for the consequences of sin. A man may be deeply remorseful over some wrong he has done when its effects become apparent, but not discontinue his sinning. Or a man may even give up some evil practice because he is fearful and afraid of the consequences. Most people mourn over some misguided act and its consequences when judgment overtakes them. Judas sorrowed over the sin of his betrayal of the Lord, but preeminently because of its evil effects (see Matt. 27:1-8). But Peter mourned over his denial of Christ because of the sin itself, and he never forgot it. David mourned over the heinous sin that he committed, not because of its effects. Psalms 32 and 51 are clear evidence of how deeply and rightly he mourned over his sins. And the real motive appears in the words of his confession: "For I acknowledge my transgressions, and my sin is ever before me. Against *thee* thee only, have I sinned" (51:3-4).

The godly, as they meditate on the Word and lean upon the Holy Spirit to teach them, as they behold in the Word the beauty, glory, holiness, and righteousness of the Lord, as they realize the wonder and blessedness of being *His,* are driven to sorrow for their sins in true contrition, and thus to full confession. David's words reveal his complete recognition of the enormity of his sins, and genuine contrition for them, and it cannot be otherwise with *us.* The presence and power of sin are evident, and if we say we have no sin, we deceive ourselves, and the truth is not in us. And if we say that we have not sinned, we make God a liar. But if we confess our sins, He is faithful and just to forgive us our sins, and to cleanse us from all unrighteousness.

It is probable this mourning would include all other griefs and sorrows due to the reality of sin and its power in the world: the blows, pains, injuries, wrongs, inequalities, inequities, and losses that are a part of the experience of this life. They are common to the human realm and we must face them and bear them. But the godly believer will mourn profoundly not only for sins that are known openly, but for secret sins—those sins that the world does not know and cannot observe. David prayed earnestly, "Cleanse thou me from *secret* faults . . . " (Ps. 19:12). Such sins will cause unutterable sorrow in the godly heart of a true Christian, to whom sin has been revealed by the light of the Word in its full and awful despicableness, against the person and presence in us of our blessed Lord. And godly sorrow, while weeping over one's own sins, will at the same time weep real tears over the sins of others in the body of Christ. It cannot help doing so.

The Significance of the Present Tense of the Verb

The substantive participle penthountes is in the present tense, indicating present, continuing action. It characterizes the mourning of the godly as that which goes on constantly. The world will never be rid of its sin; it will prevail until this age is done. So Christ's own must go on mourning. Christians must not fall into the error of believing that there may come a time in their experience when repentance and contrition are no longer warranted. It is well to be reminded of the first of Luther's famous ninety-five Theses, which testifies that our entire life is to be a continuous repentance and contrition. Great indeed is the need for those who have named the name of Christ to be awakened to the awful reality of sin, its presence, and its power. How greatly the church needs a new awareness of and sensitiveness to *sin*! How vitally necessary that believers be alive to the weakness of the human frame! David testifies, "For mine iniquities are gone over mine head; like an heavy burden they are too heavy for me" (Ps. 38:4). It is imperative that we recognize the merciless power of sin and our utter helplessness to thrust it aside and escape. Our only hope is in complete dependence upon the God of all grace. Thus our mourning is a constant and continuous cry to Him in our own distress, amid the sins of the world around us, and in the knowledge of our helplessness, and the painful consequences of our own wrongdoing.

With regard to the other griefs and sorrows, we know the testimony of the Word: "We must through much tribulation enter into the kingdom of God" (Acts 14:22b); "For unto you it is given in the behalf of Christ, not only to believe on him, but also to suffer for his sake" (Phil. 1:29); "If we suffer, we shall also reign with him" (II Tim. 2:12a); "I, John, who also am your brother, and companion in tribulation . . . " (Rev. 1:9). The saved go on mourning, but they are blessed in such a course, and comforted in their tribulation.

The Assurance in Which the Blessedness Consists

" . . . because they shall be comforted. "

hoti autoi parakleitheisontai

The Objects of this Comforting Are Emphasized.

The emphatic pronoun autoi means "they alone"—*they, they only,* shall be comforted. It is only those who mourn who need to be comforted, and it is *only they* who ever get to know what it is to be comforted. There are lulls in the storms which sweep the sea of life. There are many evidences of God's goodness in the earth. There are the blessings and comforts of home and family life, the transitory joys and successes which come, the sympathy and condolence of relatives and friends, the comfortings and releases from grief and pain which God providentially grants to all. But *only they who mourn* with the mourning here set forth ever know the comfort also revealed in this verse. The mourning brings the comforting which is never withheld. We may turn again to David as the example of one who so mourned and thus realized the blessed comfort which only the true God can give: "Thou which hast shown me great and severe troubles, shalt revive me again, and shalt bring me up again from the depths of the earth. Thou shalt increase my greatness and comfort me on every side" (Ps. 71:20-21). Psalms 31 and 32 are further illustrations. Indeed, blessed are they who mourn, for only they shall be comforted.

The Nature of the Comforting Is Shown

The verb form parakleitheisontai, from parakaleo, expresses a comforting which is blessed indeed to those who must face the realities of grief, sorrow, tribulation, and trouble. The verb means literally to "call alongside" (cf. Acts 28:20). So it may also be rendered "call for, call on, call to," which may be done in a variety of senses. The verb has in it the ideas of "admonish, exhort" (Acts 2:40; I Thess. 2:11); "beseech, entreat" (Rom. 12:1; Philem. 10); "console, encourage" (II Cor. 1:4-6; 2:7); "comfort, strengthen" (I Thess. 4:18; Eph. 6:22; Col. 4:8; II Thess. 2:16-17); "instruct, teach" (Titus 1:9). Other passages may be consulted as illustrations of the manifold use and meaning of this extraordinary word.[7]

Thus the comforting is that which only the eternal God Himself can give, the comfort brought to us by the One who Himself comes alongside to help, to succor, in answer to our cry. He is always there, beseeching, admonishing, consoling, sympathizing, encouraging, strengthening, teaching. These are the assurances of our God, whose presence is so manifested. As our mourning rises to Him in this earthly vale of sin and tears, in this manner His constant, unsurpassed comfort comes to us, and of all the comforts there is the supreme comfort without which all the rest is vain, the comfort of complete deliverance from the guilt of sin and the wonder of eternal life.

---

[7]See also the noun form parakleisis, which is used for imploration and entreaty (II Cor. 8:4); for exhortation and admonition (I Tim. 4:13); for consolation and comfort (Rom. 15:4-5; II Cor. 1:4-7).

The Agent of This Comforting Is Revealed

The passive voice of the verb (parakleitheisontai) points to the action operative upon the subject. The agent of the comforting which comes to the mourners is thus revealed. While it is true that all comforting comes from God, our Heavenly Father, as the originating Source (II Cor. 1:3), it is equally true that the Holy Spirit is the present indwelling Comforter of each believer (John 14:16-17). In this passage, the Holy Spirit is called parakleiton (one who is called alongside to help). The word is derived from the verb used in the Matthew 5:4 text (parakaleo). The Spirit's ministry is to comfort, teach, guide, keep, and intercede for the believer. Thus the parakleitos is seen as the ministering agent of the comforting indicated by the passive parakleitheisontai.

It is a blessed thing to know and to be assured of the very comfort of God. The paracletism of the Paraclete Himself is ever with us. We are not left to cry out hopelessly in the darkness, to grope desperately here and there, to suffer unbearably. The Paraclete is there, ever at hand, by our side, to make His power and presence felt, and to minister to us the comfort and help of the Holy Scriptures (Acts 9:31; II Tim. 3:16).

The Time of the Comforting Is Set Forth

The tense of the verb form parakleitheisontai is future: "they shall be comforted." Some hold that this passage is intended only for the future Messianic Kingdom, thus depriving believers of the blessed ministry of comfort in the present. The mourners must remain comfortless until the time for this future comforting comes. There is no comfort, no consolation, no relief, in the present time—now—when it is so greatly needed, only in the future when it will not be so needed.

Such teaching is certainly in error. All Scripture assures the believer of comfort now, in the present time. The Old Testament witnesses to the comforting presence of the Lord with His people, and the New Testament assures us of the same. Our Lord said, "I will not leave you comfortless: I will come to you" (John 14:18), and the writer to the Hebrews quotes Deuteronomy 31:6 to assure his readers of the blessed, comforting presence of the Lord: "For he hath said, I will never leave thee nor forsake thee" (Heb. 13:5). Moreover, we have the abiding presence of the Comforter, the Holy Spirit Himself.

The future tense is proper. The truth is precisely stated: "They shall be comforted." To every mourner, the comforting instantly comes. The future tense of the verb is future with respect to the mourning. We mourn, and then are comforted. The comforting at once follows the mourning. We may call this a progressive future (cf. Phil. 1:18; II Thess. 3:4). Blessed *now* are the mourners, for they shall at once be comforted, and it will continue to be so. It goes on like this—on into the future. The mourners are blessed for they shall be comforted. In the grand era of the Messianic Kingdom, there will be no mourning on the part of all who reign with Christ, hence no need *then* for comforting.

The Means of the Comforting Is Suggested

While there is no definite, direct mention of a specific means in this ministry of comforting, nevertheless a suggestion as to the means used is found in the verb parakleitheisontai. We recall the general meaning of the verb parakaleo, "address, speak to, call, call to, etc.," which may be done in a variety of senses: admonition, entreaty, exhortation, comfort, instruction, etc. We understand that the agent of this varied ministry of comforting is the parakleitos, the Holy Spirit, the One called alongside to help. It is His purpose to teach us all things (John 14:26), to guide us into all truth (John 16:13), and to reveal to us the deep things of God (I Cor. 2:10). The inference is plain. The means by which this ministry is carried on and accomplished can be none other than the Word of God, the very Holy Scriptures themselves. It is by means of the Word that the Holy Spirit admonishes and exhorts us, entreats and encourages us. It is in the Word that we find comfort and solace, deliverance and courage. It is with the Scriptures that we are corrected, reproved, instructed in the ways of righteousness. It is in the Word that the Holy Spirit shows us the person, power, and perfections of Christ, and reveals to us the things of God. Here, then, is the means by which this ministry of abounding comfort, in its manifold character, is exercised by the divine agent, the Holy Spirit of God. (Psalm 119 leaves us in no doubt as to this. See also: Rom. 15:4; I Thess. 2:13; 4:18; James 1:21-25; I Peter 1:23-25).

Let us say in conclusion that the second Beatitude is the complement of the first. In the words of David Brown, "The one is the intellectual, the other the emotional aspect of the same thing."[8] It is the person who is beggarly poor in spirit who confesses, "I am undone," and it is the mourning caused by the knowledge of this undone condition which issues in the cry of lamentation, "Woe is me! For I am undone!" There is a sorrow which is very lightly comforted with nothing; there is on the other hand a superstitious and proud sorrow which refuses to take comfort from the God of all grace. To all whose mourning does not spring from poverty of the spirit, this promise is most assuredly not given. But we who mourn over sin are of all people most blessed, for we are comforted. These present days of mourning are limited, and they shall shortly be ended. Even now, while being comforted, we know that we shall be with Him, and there will be no more tears, death, sorrow, or crying. Then, in the highest sense, we shall be comforted.

---

[8]*Commentary on the New Testament, Gospel of Matthew* (Hartford: S. S. Scranton Company, Publishers, n.d.), 2:17.

3

THE THIRD PRONOUNCEMENT

"Blessed [are] the meek;
for they shall inherit the earth."

(v. 5)

The Aspect of Blessedness

"Blessed [are] the meek ones. . . ."

makarioi hoi praeis

This Beatitude follows logically, for the beggarly poor in spirit who continue to mourn over sin, are quite likely to be meek. It is hardly possible that it could be otherwise.

Praeis comes from praos, which denotes that which is mild, soft, gentle. It is so used in the Greek writings, and in the New Testament, as well as in the Septuagint Version several times for ahnah and ahnee. Hoi praeis are the mild, the patient, the gentle, the tender-hearted. When they are threatened, abused, and reviled, they display no retaliatory resentment, vindictiveness, or bitterness, and so do not rush to strike back in anger and revenge. This attitude, which involves a quiet, willing, cheerful obedience and submission to God, thus stands in direct contrast to the stubborn, willful, carnal rebellion and self-assertiveness of the natural man.

Praos appears in four New Testament passages: Matthew 5:4; 11:29; 21:5; I Peter 3:4. The related praoteis is used more frequently, being found some twelve times to designate mildness, gentleness, meekness. The meek are the direct opposite of the vengeful and violent. The various forms of this word suggest an inner quality of mind which is indicative of the willingness and plasticity of spirit in opposition to the proud, unbending obstinacy of the natural self-will. Rambach, in Stier, comments:

> This is a fruit of the Spirit which is found upon the soil of spiritual poverty, contrition, and mourning; a noble flower which grows out of the ashes of self-love, upon the grave of pride. On the one hand a man sees his own utter ruin, his unworthiness and misery; on the other he contemplates the kindness and benignity of God in Christ Jesus (Titus 3:2-4). The internal characteristic is a disposition of heart, which, through the keen perception of its own misery, and of the abounding mercy of God, has become so pliant gentle, mild, flexible, and tractable, that no traces of its original ruggedness, of its wild and untamed nature remain.[9]

The contrast between a spirit of severity and violence, and that of meekness and gentleness, is well set forth in I Corinthians 4:21, "Shall I come to you with a rod . . . or . . . in the spirit of meekness?" The word is used in Galatians 6:1, where it describes the manner in which a sinning brother is to be restored ("restore such an one in the spirit of meekness . . . "). This gentle spirit is to be manifested in the life of God's ministering servants, according to I Timothy 6:11, "follow after . . . meekness." It is the same gentle spirit which is in the sight of God, of great price (I Peter 3:4), and a fruit of the Spirit (Gal. 5:22). And we cannot overlook the address of Paul to Titus (3:1-2), "Put them in mind to be subject to principalities and powers, to obey magistrates, to be ready to every good work, To speak evil of no man, to be no brawlers, but gentle, showing all meekness unto all men."

Yet it is a mistake to suppose that the meek are cowardly. The word has no such meaning, does not even suggest such a thing. Neither are they deficient in strength of purpose, force of will, or determination of duty. While they may not often be giants where physical prowess and other similar temporal capabilities are concerned, nevertheless they *are* capable of the most

---

[9]Rambach, quoted by Rudolph Stier, op. cit., p. 106.

strenuous action in behalf of others, and for the praise and glory of the Lord. Moreover they are far from being weaklings where the defense and confirmation of the Gospel are concerned, and whenever the blessed sacred truth of the Word of God is attacked and blasphemously denied. They are meek in spirit, but mighty in faith. Still, it is indeed true that too little of this meekness is often manifest among believers. As Lenski remarks:

> Our meekness however often shines by its absence, and other less desirable traits are instead seen: pride, selfishness, disobedience, neglect, etc., which necessitate divine discipline. For God does not leave us to become engrossed in mere temporalities, without His witness. His purpose and desire for His own are far loftier, higher, greater, and have their end in conformity to the image of His Son, whose words are these: "Learn of me, for I am meek and lowly in heart."[10]

The Lord, however, displayed anger on occasion. He was angry with the religionists of His day; He became angry over the legalistic formalism so prevalent; He showed anger in the synagogue where He healed the man's paralyzed hand, because of the attitude of many in attendance there that day; He was angry at the invasion of the Temple by the money-changers; He became angry with Peter; and He protested at being struck by an officer in the High Priest's court, prior to the crucifixion. Was His anger a violation of His holiness and meekness? *By no means*—the Lord became angry because of correct motivation. It was not the unreasonable anger of one whose human passion gained control and became ungovernable. Neither was it a petty anger aroused by trifling and capricious things. The denial that the Lord should ever become angry is based on the common conception of human anger, a selfish, passionate flaring-up which is sinful. But the Lord's anger was always a holy reaction against what is wrong. Men's sins, the hardness of their hearts, and resistance against the truth of the Holy Word are respon-

---

[10]Op. cit., p. 189.

sible for divine anger. Following His example, it is proper for believers to be stirred with a holy indignation, and without sinning (see Ephesians 4:26, rightly interpreted). True Christians *ought to be moved* with holy anger by any attack upon the person and doctrine of Christ, by any violation of what is holy and sacred, pure and good, by all willful and obdurate resistance of the human heart to divine truth, and by all the sinful practices of men. Raymond L. Cramer has fittingly remarked:

> To most of us the word *meek* has been given the wrong slant—a Casper Milquetoast type of personality, one who lacks intestinal fortitude and gumption, one who can be pushed around by the aggressor—is timid and withdrawn. We might have expected Jesus to conclude His first congratulation to such people as He did in the first Beatitude—"for theirs is the Kingdom of Heaven"—but to our amazement, Jesus actually promises *the meek* the empire of the solid earth. Why did Jesus put such a premium on *meekness?* The world in which we live urges us to use our potential, to specialize, to be motivated toward success. Our government is asking for selective brains, encouraging school people to locate the more capable learner—the superior student early in life and motivate him to enter the scientific field. But the individual who will inherit the earth is not necessarily *this* person, but rather the one who is *meek*. . . .[11]

Meekness is not a passive acceptance of all the sinful acts and evil practices which unsaved men may try to enforce upon us in this world. Certainly being meek involves patience, longsuffering, gentleness, and the will to refrain from retaliation. It involves the acceptance of personal affront without giving back like for like. But meekness is not grasping for peace at any cost. It is not parleying with religionists and so-called Christian leaders who deny the doctrine of Christ and question the integrity of the Holy Scriptures. It is not tacitly condoning what is wrong

---

[11]*The Psychology of Jesus and Mental Health,* (Los Angeles: Cowman Publications Inc., 1959), pp. 80-82.

when speaking out for what is right is really necessary. It is not giving in, even against odds, without declaring the truth. It is not holding back in the presence of others and allowing someone to go on suffering without offering help. It is not refusing to be merciful to a needy person surrounded by the hatred and threats of many enemies. It is anger controlled by God; it is being angry over the right things for reasons that are justifiable; it is holy indignation because the Christian cause is being blasphemed. It is knowing to do good—and doing it. Spiros Zodhiates writes:

> In a world such as ours there is a place for strife, a place for anger, for strong speech and strong action. We have no business trying to pass through a world of conflicting forces without taking sides. We are simply cowardly when, in order to save ourselves possible discomfort or unpopularity, we cautiously forbear uttering a word of censure upon some powerful evil or abuse. We cannot sympathize very strongly with the right if we see it overborne without coming forward in its defense. . . . The man who cannot be angry at evil lacks enthusiasm for good. . . . Meekness regards evil-doers as those who deserve to be blamed and to be chastised, and to feel the bitterness of their evil and not to interfere too much with the salutary laws that bring down sorrow upon men's heads if they have been doing wrong, but on the other hand it takes care that our sense of justice does not swallow up the compassion that weeps for the criminal as an object of pity. . . .[12]

Whatever further may be said of this meekness, it is an inner state, an internal attitude of mind and disposition of heart, which bows to the will of God with unquestioning submission. Inner meekness toward God works for outer meekness toward men. Perhaps the whole matter might be best explained as being controlled by God and not by self. If this is not so—how can we be pronounced *blessed*?

---

[12]*Meekness* (Ridgefield, N. J.: American Mission to Greeks, Inc., 1962), pp. 7, 33.

The Assurance in Which the Blessedness Consists

"Because they shall inherit the earth"

hoti autoi kleironomeisousin tein gein

Again we note the presence of the emphatic pronoun autoi, "only they—they alone." It is *only* these meek ones who shall inherit the earth. Again, as in the case of the beggarly poor who possess the Kingdom (v. 3), it is indeed paradoxical that people who are meek, mild, gentle, and patient shall inherit the earth. This truth reemphasizes the fact that the divine pattern and economy are completely and exactly contrary to the world order. The contrast between the meek and their humble state, and the wicked of the world with their wealth, pomp, and display, is set forth in Psalm 37:11-22, from which our Lord drew His words in this Beatitude.

In this Psalm, the state of God's believing people and the state of the unregenerate of the earth are contrasted, and the meek are cautioned not to vex themselves, nor fret, nor become impatient and overanxious when the world and its people grow haughty, arrogant, and cruel, and boast themselves as mighty, great, and prosperous. Neither are the Lord's people to lose hope when suffering comes, nor become wrathful at the world's prosperity and seek their own vindication. For the blessing of the Lord, His provision, His presence, and His power are with them *in this life, on this earth*—which actually is *theirs.* The Lord knows the days of the upright, and their inheritance shall be forever. While the wicked appear to prevail and prosper, and possess the earth, nevertheless "The Lord shall laugh at him: for he seeth that his day is coming." They shall be cut off, and the meek shall inherit the earth. "For the Lord loveth justice and forsaketh not his saints." Six times this inheritance appears by specific mention in the Psalm (vv. 9, 11, 18, 22, 29, 34).

The word for "inherit" is kleironomeisousin, from the verb kleironomeo, "to receive a lot (as an inheritance), to receive an allotted portion for one's own." It is the verb used for "inherit," in the Septuagint Version throughout Psalm 37. It appears very frequently in the Old Testament in the phrases kleironomeisousin gein and tein gein (the same sentence as the text in Matt. 5:5), when the Bible speaks of the occupation of the promised land by the Israelites (Lev. 20:24; Deut. 4:22, etc.).

The promise in these words does bring out a more immediate reference to Canaan as the promised land, the secure possession of which was to the Old Testament faithful ones the evidence of God's favor and blessing, thus reaching ahead to the restoration of the believing remnant in that land. Yet it is quite possible that there is something else here for the church: By comparing "Those that wait upon the Lord, they shall inherit the earth" (v. 9), with I Corinthians 3:21: "For all things are yours," we cannot omit the reference to the present blessing of God in this earth. For even in Psalm 37, from which the words are taken, as David Brown says, "The promise to the meek is not held forth as an arbitrary reward, but as having a kind of natural fulfillment."[13] The meek delight in the Lord, and He gives them the desires of their hearts (v. 4); they commit their way to Him and trust in Him, and He brings it to pass (v. 5); they may be oppressed, cursed, and plotted against, even slain, yet He brings forth their righteousness as the light, and never forsakes them (vv. 6, 25, 28); and the little they have of temporal goods is better than the riches of many wicked ones (v. 16). The Lord knows the days of the upright and their inheritance shall be forever, but the wicked shall perish (vv. 18, 20). The wicked may be in great power, spreading himself like a green bay tree, yet he passes away and cannot be found—but the way of the upright is peace (vv. 35-37). Transgressors rule, oppress, and even seek to do away with the children of God, yet the righteous have the promises of God, experience His delivering power, and possess salvation and eternal life (vv. 32, 39, 40).

In short, all things belong to the meek. All things are *theirs*. They possess that blessing and favor which are life, together with all the rights and privileges which are theirs in that life, of

---

[13]Op. cit., p. 18.

being sons of God by adoption. All things are theirs, whether the world, or life, or death, or things present, or things to come (I Cor. 3:21-22). At length they will overcome and inherit all things (Rev. 21:7). Hence as children of God (tekna) led by the Spirit of God, and thus sons (huioi), and if children, then heirs, heirs of God, and joint-heirs with Christ, the meek are the only rightful occupants, the only real possessors, the only legitimate owners of the earth. The meek may not now be rich in temporal goods; mighty men, the ungodly, may domineer, oppress, and increase in wealth, pomp, and power, yet the truth is that *the earth belongs to the meek ones,* for they have a rightful claim to it. To them God will grant the honor of executing upon the wicked nations and their leaders the judgment written (Ps. 149:4-9).

4

THE FOURTH PRONOUNCEMENT

"Blessed [are] they
who do hunger and thirst after righteousness;
for they shall be filled."

(v. 6)

The Aspect of Blessedness

"Blessed [are] they
who hunger and thirst after righteousness."

makarioi hoi peinontes kai dipsontes tein dikaiosunein

The beggarly poor in the spirit, in their meekness do not only mourn. They are not content to only shed tears, but they "hunger and thirst after righteousness." Out of a humbleness of soul grows the sanctified desire which aspires honestly and earnestly toward that which is *right and good.* Stier says:

> The future possessors of the earth, and its now rightfully installed heirs, whose even now is the kingdom of heaven with all its reversion, including the ruling upon earth, *hunger and thirst* throughout their whole course, even as they did at the beginning: just as the poor to whom the kingdom of heaven is imparted, mourn in the first repentance unto life which they receive as a bestowment of grace, and oftentimes after. But the Lord ever more and more comforts the mourners, ever more and more fills the hungry and thirsty soul with the good things of His righteousness.[14]

---

[14]Op. cit., p. 109.

The Expression of Desire and Need: "The ones hungering and thirsting"

Hungering and thirsting go together. They are so used to express strong spiritual desires and needs. Peinontes is from peinao, and means properly "to hunger, suffer want, be needy." (See Matt. 4:2; Rom. 12:20; Phil. 4:12.) It is so used in the Greek classics from Homer down, and in the Septuagint for rahabeh. Metaphorically, the word is used to express a "seeking with eager compelling desire." It appears in the Greek authors with the genitive of the thing sought after.[15]   However, in Matthew 5:6, it has the accusative dikaiosunein.

In this sense it is joined with dipsao, which means "to suffer thirst" (John 4:15). It has the same sense in the Greek writings. Together, peinontes and dipsontes express an ardent craving, an intense yearning, a profound sense of need. Even in the natural realm, hunger and thirst are the strongest impulses, and when they are stirred and excited, they mount and increase until they are satisfied. In the natural man there is a hunger and thirst that is not of God; it is a result of the Fall. This hunger and thirst in unregenerate man, which God did not create in him, after some brief semblance of gratification, will warrant the pain and torment of eternal famishing. The hunger and thirst of the unsaved man for the things of the world—which, except for some momentary, temporary gratification and a transitory relief, never satisfy—receives no expiation. Without God these cravings, desires, and appetites carry men to the grave and an eternal Hell, but the craving, yearning, seeking, needing wrought in the soul by the Lord are different. They constitute a hunger and thirst *for more and more of Him and His* (see Ps. 42:2; 63:1-2).

The two participles peinontes and dipsontes are in the durative present tense to show that the hungering and thirsting continue, going on and on in this life, and as Lenski comments,

---

[15]mala deinontes summachon chreimaton, Xenophon, Cyril 7,5,50; 8,3, 39.

"increases in the very act of being satisfied." The meek taste, and desire more. The desire grows, the need increases, the craving becomes more intense, and God keeps filling the hungry with good things (Luke 1:53). Daily we cry for strength and sustenance, for grace and mercy, and daily the Lord satisfies us. This is a matter of *both desire and duty*. The figure of hunger and thirst used by our Lord plainly refers to those whose deepest, innermost cravings and yearnings are for spiritual things, whose greatest desires are godly. These *will* keep on hungering and thirsting for more and more of Christ and His likeness—*it is expected* that they will do so. The present participles denote both privilege and practice. They do not, however, suggest the enthronement of hunger and thirst as ends in themselves for the sake of Christ. It is not intended that we shall go on seeking out these things as a continuing state of life in which there is glory for God and blessing for us. Hunger and thirst are not virtues which enhance the Christian life and evidence the reality of one's conversion. It is not necessary for us to go hungry and suffer thirst in order to become Christians and to be blessed by the Lord. But the figure of hunger and thirst for righteousness is superb. The hungering and thirsting for more and more of Christ and His Word *do* constitute a sign of life of the newborn man quickened out of the sleep of death. As a manner of expressing the internal spirit and disposition of those who are true children of God, it is sublime.

Attention should be called to the fact that Luke, who uses only peinontes, and omits dipsontes, yet adds significantly nun—"now." This brings out in bold relief the time during which this hungering and thirsting continues: "Blessed are ye that hunger *now*. . . ." It is *now*, in this present age, during the current time, in every generation of this era between the Advents of Christ, i.e., in His own day, during the apostolic period, throughout the history of the church, down to the present time, and terminating in His *return*. It is clear then, that the blessedness concerns *us*. *We* seek after righteousness now, the victory of the eternal, the just and good will of God upon earth and in humanity, especially, however, in ourselves. We pray "Deliver *us* from evil!" But *first* we cry "Hallowed be *Thy* name! *Thy* will be done!" And we receive the daily bread, for our bodies and for our souls.

The Essence of the Desire and Need

It is quite obvious that tein dikaiosunein, "the righteousness," does not refer to regeneration, as some infer, for these Beatitudes are pronounced upon people whose character has already been designated as makarioi. The hunger and thirst marked out here come only after we are saved. Rare indeed is the case of a man—if indeed there are any cases at all—who hungers and thirsts for God prior to salvation. But neither does dikaiosunein refer to the power of right and justice in human affairs, as some interpret. Nor does it designate a virtue which enables all men to "live right and do good." The very nature of the passage forbids this, as does the verb "shall be filled."

The word dikaiosunei may be taken in two general senses. In the *broad* sense, it indicates *the state of one who is such as he ought to be*—that condition approved and acceptable to God. It thus denotes that state acceptable to God which is granted to the sinner who receives the grace, by faith, offered to him in the expiatory death of the Lord Jesus Christ on the cross (Rom. 4:5). It also refers to that integrity and purity of desire and life, that uprightness and correctness of thinking, feeling, and acting, which constitutes the new experience of the saved man (Rom. 6:13, 16, 18-20; Phil. 1:11). When affirmed of Christ Himself, the word denotes His perfect moral purity, integrity, and sinlessness (John 16:8, 10; I John 2:1); and of God, His holiness (Rom. 3:5, 26). In a *closer* sense, the word indicates that virtue which gives each one his due, i.e., justice. This is said to belong to God and to Christ (II Peter 1:1; Rom. 9:28).

We repeat, dikaiosunein is not to be taken here in the sense of salvation from sin. Certainly it is the state into which the sinner enters, and the possession he (she) is granted at the moment of regeneration. But this is not the sense in which the word is used here. Rather, it must be taken in its aspect of integrity and purity of desire and life which inspires and dominates the Christian's purpose and practice. It involves the ever-increasing sense of need for the Lord, the realization that without Him we are nothing. It describes the craving to know more of Him, the yearning to be more like Him, the compelling desire to live purer, holier, firmer, more effective lives before men, and the resolve by the grace of God to do so. Yearning to be more like the Saviour is the chief virtue of Christian character (Phil. 1:9-11; 3:8-9; Rom. 13:14).

Augustine said that the mourners hunger and thirst after the Righteous One—"Jesus Christ the Righteous." They were made for Him, and will never be satisfied until they attain to the fruition of all their hopes, to know *Him* and the power of His resurrection and the fellowship of His sufferings.

We concur in this remark by Augustine, for the definite article particularizes the noun, and points to the One in whom all righteousness is to be found. It is in the knowledge of Him that the saved come to know more and more of that righteousness which is by faith. Without doubt such will be their supreme motive and desire, and in this the various other aspects of their hungering and thirsting after righteousness will be fulfilled. They will hunger and thirst for constant growth in grace and daily triumph over the agencies of the world and the lusts of the flesh. They will hunger and thirst for purer motives and greater effectiveness in witnessing and serving. They will hunger and thirst for the great, ultimate triumph of righteousness in their own hearts now, in this world of men (Gal. 5:5). The hungry and thirsty ones look and long for the return of the Lord and the triumph of His Kingdom, for "the work of righteousness shall be peace; and the effect of righteousness, quietness and assurance forever" (Isa. 32:17).

The Assurance in Which the Blessedness Consists

". . . because they only shall be filled,"

hoti autoi chortastheisontai

Four significant truths appear in these tremendously assuring and sustaining words which form this clause, with respect to the filling promised.

It Is a Filling which Thoroughly Fills and Completely Satisfies.

The verb chortastheisontai, "shall be filled," is a strong word, derived from chortadzo, used uniformly in the earlier Greek writings to express the feeding, filling, and fattening of animals with fodder and grain. In later Greek, both classical and Biblical, it denotes the filling and satisfying of men with an abundance of food.[16]

The word assures us of filling that is real, abundant, and completely satisfying. William Nast states:

> This must not be understood as if this hunger and thirst would ever cease in this world, but each new sensation of hunger and thirst will be removed by a corresponding new measure of the desired food. The perfect fullness, however, shall not be received before the resurrection of the body. . . . On the new earth, where righteousness dwelleth, we shall neither hunger nor thirst any more.[17]

Read Psalm 104 for a description of the completeness and abundance of God's filling. Psalm 107:9 states: "For He satisfieth the longing soul, and filleth the hungry soul with goodness." And we may further rejoice and be even more greatly

---

[16]It appears in the Septuagint Version for sabayah and yisebayah. *Prop.*, see Matt. 15:33; John 6:26; James 2:16, etc. *Meta.*, it is used in the text, and in Luke 6:21.

[17]*A Commentary on the Gosepl of Matthew* (New York: Carlton and Lanahan, Publishers, 1870), p. 246.

encouraged and assured by the words in Psalm 34:10, "But they that seek the Lord shall not [lack] any good thing." The Hebrew verb rendered "want" in some versions is the same word that is found in Psalm 23:1, "I shall not *want*," (chahsar), and means "fail, lessen, abate, fall off." Those who seek the Lord, the meek ones who mourn over sin and who hunger and thirst after righteousness, shall not only be filled and satisfied with all good things, but may be assured that nothing of these good things shall fail to them, the divine supply will not lessen, God's provision will not abate, fall off, decline in its sufficiency. David says, "My cup runneth over. Surely goodness and mercy shall follow me all the days of my life . . . " (Ps. 23:5-6). Bishop Ryle remarks: "Blessed are all such! They shall have enough one day. They shall 'awaken after God's likeness and be satisfied' " (Ps. 17:15).[18]

It Is a Filling which Comes Only to Those Who Hunger and Thirst After Righteousness.

We have noted the presence of the emphatic pronoun autoi in verses 4, 5. Hence it remains simply to call attention to it briefly here, and observe that such abundance of fullness and satisfaction, the blessedness of this filling from the hand of God, can never be known except through the experience of hungering and thirsting for it. People of the world know nothing of this. They hunger and thirst, but not for the living God. The gratification of their desires, the satisfying of their hunger and the quenching of their thirsting, are but momentary, not lasting, never enduring. Doubtless there are many Christians whose experience of Christ has not been high, and thus they go on through this life, never realizing the complete blessedness of fullness in the Lord, never experiencing the wonder of such intimate fellowship with Christ, for they have never really hungered and thirsted after righteousness. Therefore, they have

18*Expository Thoughts on the Gospels, Matthew-Mark* (Grand Rapids: Zondervan Publishing House, 1951), 1:33.

never known this filling. It is somewhat like the stanza of the following poem:

> Heaven above is softer blue,
> Earth around is sweeter green;
> Something shines in every hue,
> Some Christian eyes have never seen.

It Is a Filling which Has its Source in God Himself.

The passive voice of the verb chortastheisontai shows that He— God Himself—is the great and blessed source of all the good things, of the complete filling. "Every good gift and every perfect gift is from above, and cometh down from the Father of lights, with whom there is no variableness, neither shadow of turning" (James 1:17). "The earth is full of the goodness of the Lord" (Ps. 33:5). "Blessed be the Lord, who daily loadeth us with benefits" (Ps. 68:19). "And My people shall be satisfied with my goodness, saith the Lord" (Jer. 31:14). This is a fundamental truth with a large practical side, which needs to be reiterated again and again. All we are and all we have comes from above, from our Father in heaven. We must be reminded constantly that the sole source of blessedness is the eternal God Himself. The satisfaction of the hungering and thirsting after righteousness comes only from the Lord. Let us not waste time seeking knowledge of God, Christian maturity, and spiritual strength and success in any other realm than that which is heavenly, or from any source than the Lord Jesus Christ, for in Him is all the fullness of the Godhead bodily (Col. 2:9), and we are full in Him.

It Is a Filling which Is Assured Now, and for all Time Ahead.

Once again the future tense verb is to be noted, chortastheisontai, but as in the case of the comforting of verse 4, we cannot accept this as a far-distant future, a time reserved for the Millennial Era, or in heaven. The verb matches the figure and action expressed by the hungering and thirsting. To thrust the filling into a remote future is to strip us of all hope of such satisfaction in the present time—when it is so greatly needed. We understand clearly that only when we are with the Lord, reigning with Him, joined to Him forever, will we realize the blessedness of complete and perfect fullness and satisfaction. Yet it is possible to know the satisfaction of belonging to Him who at once feeds the hungry and gives drink to the thirsty.

We must recall Luke's "now"—"Blessed are ye that hunger now. . . ." Are we blessed *now* when we hunger and thirst after righteousness, yet find no satisfaction in the present, but learn that we must wait until we have reached heaven before we shall be fed and filled? The whole teaching of the Scriptures is against this idea. As we hunger and thirst after righteousness *now,* we are fed, comforted, and filled *now.* And we go on, with every breath lifting up to the Lord the earnest and persistent plea: "Thy Kingdom come! . . . Come quickly, Lord Jesus!" Because we long for the time when there shall be no more tears, no more death, neither sorrow, nor crying, neither any more pain, when we shall be finally and everlastingly perfect and complete.

5

THE FIFTH PRONOUNCEMENT

*"Blessed [are] the merciful;
for they shall obtain mercy."*

(v. 7)

The Aspect of Blessedness

"Blessed [are] the merciful ones . . . "

makarioi hoi eleeimones

Up to this point, the Beatitudes have revealed a certain correspondence to conditions, and in each case that which is promised
is essentially a *gift*. At the same time, it must be noticed that
there is a contrast also—the "beggarly poor in spirit" receive the
Kingdom; the "meek" inherit the earth. So there is, paradox-
ically, both a correspondence between condition and cure, and
a contrast between need and fulfillment. Here, in the fifth
pronouncement, it is *the merciful obtaining mercy*. As Cramer
remarks:

> It is as though we cannot receive mercy without first giving it. It
> is a reciprocal action. It is a sobering thought that other people
> can keep us from experiencing mercy by failing to show us
> mercy. We can rob someone else of mercy by withholding mer-
> cy.[19]

Now begins the unfolding of a somewhat new series of
endeavors. However, it does not presuppose the end of the

---

[19]Op. cit., p. 139.

former. Rather, we see the beginnings of those previous inner principles as they are expressed outwardly—the fruits of those first axioms manifesting themselves now simultaneously in the life. So they who "in their poverty acknowledge their need of mercy, and taste the first-fruits of divine compassion, already begin to exercise mercy; the mourners begin while they mourn, to wash their hearts clean; the meek also spontaneously to make peace; the hungerers after righteousness to give themselves up to persecution on account of that righteousness. . . ."[20]

Luther rightly said that in all the Beatitudes, faith is pre-supposed "as the tree on which all the fruit of blessedness grows." Hence this mercy does not refer to the natural emotion found occasionally among men, but to that mercy which grows out of a personal experience of the great, unequaled mercy of God. This is spoken of those, and is intended for those, who have already experienced that mercy of God in their hearts and souls—"you who were dead in trespasses and sins. . . . But God who is rich in mercy . . . hath made us alive together with Christ . . . " (Eph. 2:1, 4-5). The new life in, and *with,* Christ initiates a learning process, a new experience of growing, developing, maturing, acquiring, in terms of new reactions, different charac-teristics, fresh attitudes, changed habits. Because of this won-drous divine dynamic, we begin to express and to extend the quality of mercy. In fact, all of the Beatitudes, with their conditions, are in a sense found in every true child of God, with differing capacity. No member of this wonderful family of graces may be altogether wanting from the time that the initial poverty of spirit has received the gift of mercy, yet there is a real and gradual, ever-advancing growth of one out of the other. But caution enters here, for the gifts received must be pre-served, exercised, and increased, for to him who has shall more be given in order to his having all, while from him who does not exercise care and increase the gifts, shall be taken away that which he has.

The plural noun eleeimones comes from eleeo, "to have mercy on, to succor the afflicted, give help to the wretched,

---

[20]Stier, op. cit., p. 111.

rescue the miserable." As is obvious from the verbal idea, the sense of the word is the expression of sympathy and compassion which manifests itself in positive action toward those who are needy. It involves the readiness to give help, the constraint which comes from a desire to relieve the suffering of others. It is not, however, that weak and sickly sympathy which carnal selfishness manages to feel, but does not reach out to succor the neighbor in need. Nor is it the false kindness toward others which goes hand in hand with the indulgence of one's own flesh. Neither is it the silent, impassive kind of pity which, while perhaps genuine in many, cannot extend itself to help in tangible ways. It is that feeling of kindness and sympathy for the miserable and afflicted which is joined with the constraining desire to relieve them, and which issues in the action of going to the aid of the needy one. It is undoubtedly true that all of us do not possess the means to help many who are in need, hence can only be pressed in heart with compassion and constraint to pray for the afflicted ones. But there are some who are able both to feel sympathy with the misery of another and to extend to that person the help he needs. Let us not forget that we have been the recipients of God's mercy which was extended to us when we stood in desperate need of something more than mere compassion lying dormant in God's heart.

The plural noun, then, describes those who have already been dealt with in mercy by the God whose mercy is plenteous. They are thus able to show mercy themselves. God first deals with us in mercy, then makes us merciful, then blesses us for being merciful, "Blessed are the merciful ones. . . ." This mercy is an outgrowth of God's mercy in us, a marked characteristic of the active side of the spiritual life. It simply follows, with all reasonableness, that we who have obtained mercy must show mercy, must ourselves be merciful toward others. Luke 6:36 says, "Be ye therefore merciful, as your Father is also merciful."

The merciful ones not only bear the insults of evil men, but their hearts go out in compassion for those wicked ones, for they know that the ungodly shall perish. The merciful are sympathetic with the afflicted, gentle to the weak, considerate of the fallen, generous toward the poor, gracious to the offender, helpful to the needy, concerned for the sin-sick. They remember the mercy bestowed upon them, and have not forgotten that they have been purged from their old sins. So they are quick to forgive and show themselves merciful to others with cheerfulness. They know that the real neighbor is the man who shows mercy to another who has been struck down. They know also that he who shows no mercy shall have judgment without mercy, and that mercy rejoices over judgment. The righteousness for which they hunger and thirst and which satisfies their cravings, yet leads them to yearn for more and will lead them to exercise mercy toward others because it has first been shown to them.

The world stands desperately in need of mercy, for the world is sick, and its people need the ministration of the great Physician who has prescribed the cure and brought it within the reach of all. Mercy offers forgiveness of sins, and this is the heart of man's need. The guilt of sins is beyond the ability of humankind to meet, but Christ will release any man who turns to Him in genuine faith from the awful imprisonment of unforgiven sins. He will dismiss the guilt and impart the assurance that the sins have been taken away forever. God's forgiveness is complete, and it is essential that men and women know that He never acts capriciously. To every individual who turns honestly to God for succor and help, the divine promise comes: "None of his sins that he hath committed shall be mentioned unto him . . . " (Ezek. 33:16a), and; "As the heavens are high above the earth, so great is his mercy toward them that fear him. As far as the east is from the west, so far hath he removed our transgressions from us" (Ps. 103:11-12). So forgiveness is inherent in the meaning of mercy. As we realize the wonder of relying upon Christ for acceptance and forgiveness, it will be easier for us to extend a kind spirit and the feeling of mercy to others. In doing so we learn the true quality of forgiveness.

We may add that it is surely worthy of observation that the apostle Paul includes mercy in the salutation of each of the

Pastoral Epistles. None of the other epistles, except II John and Jude, include mercy in their introduction. This is, without doubt, divine indication of the fact that, of all the saints, those who are true and faithful servants of Christ are most in need of mercy. At the same time they are expected to be first in manifesting mercy to others.

The Assurance in Which the Blessedness Consists

". . . because just these shall obtain mercy."

hoti autoi eleeitheisontai

The emphatic pronoun again appears to stress the fact that it is those who exercise mercy who shall also receive mercy. Only they (autoi) shall get to know the fullness of God's mercy. It is certain that "the merciful man doeth good to his own soul" (Prov. 11:17a). Cramer comments.

> Each person will literally get back what he gives. This is an automatic law of life. As a matter of fact, the merciful are too aware of their own sins to deal with another in sharp condemnation. Because they are themselves merciful, they are not so apt to arouse harsh feelings or awaken enmities. They receive what they give.[21]

Eleeitheisontai assures merciful believers that they shall be the recipients of mercy. We must again take the future tense as related to their showing mercy. As we show mercy, letting it be actively manifest toward others who are in need, we at once receive mercy. It must surely be clear that the future tense does not have its explanation and fulfillment in the Kingdom period, nor in heaven, for there will be no misery there to call out mercy. But it is *now*, in the present time, that we stand in need. There is never a moment of our lives in which we are not in need of mercy, both at the hands of our fellows, and above all,

---

[21]Op. cit., p. 139.

from the hand of God. Again and again David cried, "Be merciful to me, O God, be merciful unto me!" (see Ps. 56:1; 57:1, etc.). In Psalm 86:3, he pleads, "Be merciful to me, O Lord, for I cry unto thee *daily.*" David realized a present, daily need for mercy, and he knew that "with the Lord there is mercy" (Ps. 130:7). There is not one of us, not one of the redeemed, who does not, at some time or other, need to appropriate the words of David, and cry out to God, "O Lord . . . in the multitude of thy mercy, hear me . . . " (Ps. 69:13).

The saved will go back in their thinking, to the time when they first experienced the mercy of God, to that time when they were rescued from the path of sin and delivered from its curse and consequences. From that time forward, they are fully aware that the Lord "who daily loadeth us with benefits" does not forget that His children need His mercy. They cannot go through a day without it, and He assures them of granting mercy in the fullest measure, pressed down and running over. "My cup runneth over. . . . Surely goodness and mercy shall follow me all the days of my life. . . ." Moreover the place for obtaining this mercy has been established and set before us, to which we are admonished to keep coming, "Let us, therefore, come boldly unto the throne of grace, *that we may obtain mercy,* and find grace to help in time of need" (Heb. 4:16).

The agent back of the passive voice, "shall obtain mercy," is, of course, God Himself, whose great heart of love, sympathy, and compassion goes out to us in the manifestation of this blessed mercy. It is He who is "rich in mercy" (Eph. 2:4), and "that showeth mercy" (Rom. 9:16). Even that merciful treatment we receive at the hands of our fellow-believers has its source in Him, bestowed upon us by means of their instrumentality. The mercy of unsaved men in the world around us, as Lenski remarks, is "disjoined from Christ, relieving only physical distress."[22] This, too, is an indirect result of Christianity and the preaching of the Word, not merely an outgrowth of the natural, unregenerate heart. Psalm 119:64 testifies that the

---

[22]Op. cit., p. 191.

earth is full of the mercy of the Lord, and men cannot help but be influenced by it.

Mercy does not make us lax and careless where sin is concerned. Rather it has the result of leaving us more sensitive to it, more aware of its awfulness, its enormity. Mercy rejoices—and humbles—the heart. It stimulates our faith and subdues our proud spirit. God's mercy and truth concur—the one is never, can never be, divorced from the other. Mercy will never sacrifice truth on the altar of expediency. So David could lift up his voice to say, "But Thou, O Lord, art a God full of compassion, and gracious, longsuffering, and plenteous in mercy and truth. . . . Be merciful to me *according to thy word*" (Ps. 86:15; 119:58b).

6

THE SIXTH PRONOUNCEMENT

*"Blessed [are] the pure in heart;
for they shall see God."*

(v. 8)

The Aspect of Blessedness

"Blessed [are] the pure in heart . . . "

makarioi hoi katharoi tei kardia

This point of teaching logically follows, for there is nothing greater to impel us to honesty and purity of heart than the mercy of the eternal God. But the state of heart and life described by this Beatitude is not popular in today's modern world. The chastity expressed by purity of heart is considered to be old-fashioned, out of date, too rigidly scrupulous for an age such as this. Those who adhere to such standards are "establishment-minded," and much too morally austere to understand the needs of the present generation and the new modes of living. Cramer's comment is to the point when he says:

> Purity is not an attractive connotation; it represents some vague accomplishment that is synonymous with a puritanical, out-moded virtue. Purity seems flat, insipid, pedestrian, and dull while a slight mixture of wickedness seems spicy and intriguing. In our day we tend to desire to be good the easy way. The attitude of many toward purity might be summed up in the couplet:

> Won't somebody give me some good advice
> On how to be naughty—and still be nice?[23]

However, the word katharoi itself leaves no doubt as to its meaning. It strikes the death knell for the promiscuity of today's new morality. Katharoi comes from katharidzo, the Hellenistic form for kathairo, "to cleanse from filth and impurity." In the moral sense, it means "to free from the defilement of sin," hence, "to purify." The noun katharos (here, the plural katharoi) is akin to the Latin "castus, in-cestus" and the English word *chaste,* and is used in the Septuagint Version, mostly for tahore. The word has reference in medical terminology to a "cathartic," a purgative for the purpose of cleansing out, flushing out (catharsis), making pure. The word has the definite article hoi, and while hoi is not as strong as autoi, nevertheless it does supply a certain emphasis and gives particular significance to these katharoi. They are not people in general who call themselves "pure," nor are they such as declare that they no longer sin. No thought of perfectionism can be pressed into this articular plural noun, nor does the expression convey any idea of a morality that goes with law-works and self-righteousness. It excludes completely the assumed piety of the professing Christian, the formalism of the religionist, and shuts out all unsaved. It is not merely to be pure in the typically Levitical sense, not merely of clean hands in a Pharisaical or carnally moral sense, but in the inner being before God, who desires truth in the inward parts (Ps. 51:6). The word, with its article, describes those who have been saved, whose inner nature has been renovated, who have been washed in the Lamb's blood, and thus cleansed and delivered from the guilt of sin. Hence they have become more and more sensitive to sin, quick to discern the symptoms of impurity and defilement and to turn from them. And what is more, they will have a great, growing, compelling desire to be led only in paths that are righteous, lest some taint of uncleanness cast a shadow upon the

---

[23]Op. cit., pp. 173-174.

name and person of Him who bore their sins in His own body on the tree, and after whose steps they now follow.

The articular noun in the dative case shows the connection between the two words katharoi ("pure") and kardia ("heart"). It is a purity which is related to the heart. How forcefully this marks the great difference between real inward piety and holiness, and the ritualism and external morality of mere religion! A comparison of Old Testament Scripture reveals the fact that God required the same virtue in His people in those days. For the exact counterpart to katharoi tei kardia appears in such passages as Psalm 24:4, "He that hath . . . *a pure heart*"; 51:10, "Create in me *a clean heart* O God . . . "; 73:1, " . . . to such as are of *a clean heart*." See also Psalm 125:4, "Do good, O Lord . . . to those who are *upright in their hearts*." In the New Testament, we may compare II Timothy 2:22, "Follow righteousness . . . with them that call on the Lord out of *a pure heart*"; I Peter 1:22, "Love one another with *a pure heart* fervently." This purity of heart begins with the heart being sprinkled from an evil conscience, a heart purified by faith, in which the peace of Christ rules, and thus able to think on pure things. Stier says:

> The heart is purified through faith (Ac. 15:9); and in love out of a pure heart (I Tim. 1:5), in faith working by love, to the perfection of which faith works co-operate (Jas. 2:22), the purified heart goes on to the consummation of purity. The stimulant and impulse of practical mercy is the mercy of the Pure One towards my yet impure heart; the more diligently I now wash my heart in this mercy of God, and my hands by exercising it in return towards my neighbor, the more fully the sentiment of love within me is confirmed by the acts of love; so much the nearer do I come in the way of a priestly entrance into the Holiest. . . .[24]

From the point of the initial purifying of regeneration onward, the believer is responsible for maintaining, by the grace of God, a life of practical purity in this impure world-age, which is

---

[24]Op. cit., pp. 113-114.

Satan's domain. The inner man is the vital and vulnerable part of us, and our hearts and minds are the focal point of attack by the prince of this age and his evil forces. Evil pressures and influences are constantly being brought to bear upon our inner selves by the archenemy of God for the specific purpose of corrupting our thinking and destroying the purity of heart taught by the Lord in this Beatitude. For Satan knows full well that unclean thoughts and evil imaginations produce degradation of life. The unclean heart is described by Christ Himself in Matthew 15:19, "For out of the heart proceed evil thoughts, murders, adulteries, fornications, thefts, false witness, blasphemies. These are the things which defile a man. . . ."[25]

We cannot always prevent an evil thought from flashing into our consciousness—without any invitation or warning, suddenly it is there in all of its ugliness. But we can and must act to dispel it. We can call instantly upon the Lord to judge it and cast it out, then confess it and receive the cleansing promised by God (I John 1:9). Moreover special provision for believers has already been made by God for the protection of the inner man and the prevention of disaster to our hearts and minds. The armor described in Ephesians 6:11-18 must always be worn, and the great divine prescription and preventive of Philippians 4:6-7 is vital to our purity of heart and peace of mind. This divine provision is absolutely essential to the purity of heart at the center of the new life as it is manifested through the thoughts, emotions, feelings, desires, purposes, endeavors, and practices. As true believers wait expectantly for the Lord to come, such purity of heart and its resultant holiness of life will be evident in their daily conversation and conduct. "And every man that hath this hope [of the Lord's appearing] in him, *purifieth himself,* even as he is pure" (I John 3:3).

25P. C. Barker, in *Pulpit Commentary,"Gospel of Matthew"* (New York: Funk & Wagnalls Co., 1944), 1:192, says: "Human passions and desires of the flesh are the worst foes to the spirit. Into the heart contaminated by entertaining such guests, higher and purer cannot, will not come. Purity of heart must mean first of all pure thoughts, pure desires, pure affections."

The Assurance in Which the Blessedness Consists

" . . . because just these shall see God."

As the lack, or absence, of the thoughts and things, delusions and defilements of the flesh and the world marks the character and conduct of the saved, so is God's reward of grace to them: " . . . just they shall see God." The emphatic pronoun autoi, in accord with its previous usage, tells us that only those who are pure in heart will ever see God. As the comforting comes only to those who mourn, and as the filling with righteousness is realized only by those who hunger and thirst after it, just so only those who possess this purity of heart ever realize the blessedness of seeing God.

Let us not misunderstand—as many have done—the meaning of the words "shall see God." While it is true that the verb opsontai does signify "to see with the eyes," we know, of course, that we shall not in the literal sense see God in this present life. Still, on the other hand, to see God is not reserved only for an age to come. The pure in heart *do see Him now.* Inward purity is rewarded with inward vision. Stier says,

> Just as far as we are inwardly and essentially purified as God is pure, are we capable of living perception of Him. But that perception when perfect in the glorified, shall be also the actual vision of God; that is, be it understood, of the face of God in the Son. . . .[26]

The words of our Lord Jesus Christ recorded in John 14:19 are particularly blessed and assuring: "Yet a little while, and the world seeth me no more; *but ye see me. . . .*" The seeing on the part of the world is simply physical sight, and as our Lord was preparing for the redemptive work, after which He would depart from the earthly presence of His own, He places the vision of His disciples over against that of the world: *"Ye do see me."*

---

[26]Op. cit., p. 114.

In the nature of the case, and because of the obviously strong contrast here, the seeing on the part of those who belong to Christ is a seeing accomplished only with spiritual eyes—an inner sight that is not physical. *Yet it is definitely seeing God.* The verb tenses are present, carrying on forward indefinitely. The heart sprinkled from an evil conscience has light within with which to see the God of light and life. B. C. Caffin remarks,

> Purity of heart cleanses the mental vision; the pure in heart see mysteries of grace, mysteries of love and holiness which are hidden from the eyes of the unclean.[27]

Seeing God is the inward sight of fellowship and communion born of experience. It is the experience of those who are newly born, i.e., regenerated by the Holy Spirit with the Word. Those who thus undergo complete inward change see God by means of intimate fellowship with Him, because the heart—the inner man—is at peace with Him, being reconciled to Him. We have become His children, we now know Him as our Father, and we are conscious of His person and presence through His Spirit who is in us. Seeing God is desiring and understanding His will, which gives meaning and purpose of life. As Cramer says:

> Seeing God answers the human equation, bringing a sense of belonging and security, the ability to fit life into meaningful patterns, to solve its riddles. Not to see God is to fail to find the meaning of life. . . . Seeing God is becoming acquainted with Him, sensing His acceptance, comprehending what it means to be forgiven and made over. . . . The pure in heart are aware of a reality which most people miss. They are sure of God. . . . The pure in heart see God in the world around them while others are blind to His workings; the pure in heart are conscious of His leading in their lives even in the midst of pain and disappointment, when others are rebellious or despairing. In fact, to the

---

[27]*Pulpit Commentary*, Gospel of Matthew (New York: Funk and Wagnalls Co., 1944), 1:174.

pure in heart even adverse circumstances seem to sharpen their vision of God, so that they do not succumb to a neurotic reaction of chaos and confusion.[28]

It is true that the pure in heart see God in His Word, by faith which is, as F. B. Meyer remarks, "the almost *viva voce* utterance of Himself." In the Word the wonders of His grace and marcy are revealed, the arm of His power is stretched forth beside us, and the blessed fact of His love is poured out to us. In the Word we learn how to walk in fellowship with Him, "in the light as he is in the light." We learn how to live so that the Holy Spirit may magnify the Son of God in us, how to live the only kind of life that counts and lasts, and glorifies God. But "whosoever sinneth *hath not seen him,* neither known him" (I John 3:6). The verb "sinneth" (present participle, hamartanon) is to be taken in the sense of continuance in an habitual course of action. III John 11 says, "but he that doeth evil [practices evil, continues persistently in that course] *hath not seen* God." Those who keep to the path of sin and continue in the course of this world, fulfilling the desires of the flesh and of the mind, are by nature the children of wrath and will perish with the way of the ungodly, never having seen God at all. John 3:36 says they "shall not see life" (ouk opsontai dzoein).

Whatever further might be said with regard to seeing God in spiritual communion and fellowship with Him in the present, and seeing Him in His Word as we submit to the Spirit's administration of that Word in our life, the future verb opsontai unquestionably does carry on forward to that time of actual fulfillment when the people of God shall see the Lord and be with Him forever. "We shall be like him; for we shall see him as he is" (I John 3:2). Job reached great heights by inspiration when he said, "For I know that my redeemer liveth . . . in my flesh shall I see God; Whom I shall see for myself, and mine eyes shall behold, and not another . . . " (Job 19:25-27). David also looked to that time: "As for me, I will behold thy face in

---

[28]Op. cit., pp. 179-180.

righteousness . . . " (Ps. 17:15). Paul reached out to this time: "For now we see in a mirror darkly; but then, face to face . . . " (I Cor. 13:12).

The pure in heart eagerly await this time—or *should be* doing so—for it will come, as the Lord has promised. The fellowship of God, who is pure, with His children, the pure in heart, will be consummated in heaven and perpetuated throughout all eternity. When we look upon God, it is the Lamb of God whom we shall see. He appears in the beginning of the Revelation as we are to think of Him now and as He will appear when we see Him. He is in the midst of the Throne of Glory in the great redemption scene set forth in Revelation 5. He is the One before whom the redeemed fall down in worship and adoration and with whom they shall reign. Revelation closes with the same glorious picture of the Lamb of God: the crucified, living Saviour, true Man, and sovereign God.

To this the Beatitude attests with the articular noun ton theon, which is placed before the verb for emphasis. The pure in heart shall see *the* God, the God who is different and distinct from all other so-called gods. He is not some common, ordinary God, not the God of the rationalists, philosophers, and modernists, not the God of the liberal theologians and their followers. He is not an armchair God who can be pulled and pushed about as men please, but *the one and only true, living God,* who has revealed Himself in nature and creation, in the conscience of man, in the abundance of His goodness in the earth, in the blessed Holy Scriptures, and in the Person of His only-begotten Son, Jesus Christ, our Lord and our God.

7

THE SEVENTH PRONOUNCEMENT

"Blessed [are] the peacemakers;
for they shall be called the sons of God."

(v. 9)

The Aspect of Blessedness

"Blessed [are] the peacemakers. . . ."

makarioi hoi eireinopoioi

It naturally follows that the pure in heart are the peacemakers, for those who are themselves at peace with God will not rest satisfied so long as others are still alienated from God and not at peace with Him. Eireinopoioi is used in the Greek writings to designate "peacemakers," as rendered by the Authorized Version. The definite article hoi indicates and identifies a particular group of peacemakers—*the* peacemakers. Here is no political congress, no international board, no League of Nations, no religious order, no church embassage, no World Council. It speaks of those whose peace with God is an accomplished fact (Rom. 5:1), who live in peace, if at all possible, with all men (Rom. 12:18), who work to make and keep peace wherever peace is threatened or lost (Rom. 14:17-19), and who are intent upon following their Prince of Peace (I Peter 2:21). Stier writes:

> It is the last description of the high aim of discipleship, beyond which there is no higher step to be taken, for this makes the disciple as his Lord. Not merely are they contrasted with those who are contentious (Rom. 2:8), not merely do they keep and

preserve peace, as much as in them lies, with every man, but they make, they mediate peace, they bring and offer to the world out of the treasure of a pure heart, the peace of God![29]

The business and work of every true Christian is to occupy the divinely ordained place of *peacemaker*. However, in consideration of the extreme tensions and pressures in the present world order, this role of peacemaker seems almost impossible to fulfill. When the greatest statesmen in the world, together with others skilled in leadership, diplomacy, and governing the affairs of nations have been unable to bring peace to humankind, how can we qualify as peacemakers and succeed in our mission of peacemaking? Cramer states:

Ever since the days of the prophet Jeremiah, people have cried "Peace, peace, when there is no peace." Our generation has never known peace on a world-wide basis. During most of our history the air has been filled with rumblings of pending war until today at the so-called peak of scientific enlightenment, the menace of a global conflict threatens our atomic age with suicide. The uncertainty of being constantly on the brink of the outbreak of hostilities first on this front and then on that has a crippling effect psychologically. It infiltrates the very atmosphere we breathe. The spector of a destruction so powerful as to wipe out civilization in a single stroke hovers over us constantly. There never was a time when peace was more imperative than now. This Seventh Beatitude is as up-to-date as if it had been written today. While the tense world situation implies that what the world needs most is peace between nations, there is a necessity for cessation of hostilities on another front—one which is even more significant than the present international crisis. The need for inner peace and contentment transcends even a need for peace between nations. It is to obtaining peace in this area that the Seventh Beatitude refers. No man can become a peacemaker until he has found peace within his innermost self.[30]

---

[29]Op. cit., p. 114.
[30]Op. cit., pp. 212-213.

Hence the saved are the only ones who know what real peace is and the value of possessing it. They, therefore, are best fitted to act as the messengers of peace in this age, seeking to persuade men toward repentance and reconciliation with God—and even to bring about peace between men when and where possible. We are assured of the presence and power of the God of peace (Rom. 15:13, 33), and we are constrained to let the peace of Christ rule in our own hearts. "Endeavoring to keep the unity of the Spirit in the bond of peace" (Eph. 4:3) is our duty, and it is the particular responsibility of the servant of the Lord to "follow . . . peace . . . with them that call on the Lord out of a pure heart" (II Tim. 2:22). We are specifically instructed with reference to behavior in, and the policy of, the church, that "God is not the author of confusion, but of peace . . . " (I Cor. 14:33). Stress is laid upon our attitude toward others, for again in Hebrews 12:14 Christians are admonished to "follow peace with all men."

However we are not called upon to sacrifice *truth* for peace, and thus make the latter "peace at any price." Such peace is not really peace, because it forsakes the duty of contending for the faith once for all delivered unto the saints (Jude 3) and abandons principle, conviction, and doctrine. True peacemakers do not cry "Peace!" when there is no peace. They do not preach a spurious peace that covers over sin and does not remove it. Lenski remarks,

> These are not unionistic peacemakers who combine contrary doctrines by agreeing to disagree. Truth of God comes first, peace with men second.[31]

Our Lord said, "Suppose ye that I am come to give peace on earth? I tell you, Nay, but rather division" (Luke 12:51). This leaves no room for weakness and compromise. The Christian who enters the conflict for truth and combats error and falsehood shall not rightfully be called a divider, a disturber, a

---

[31]Op. cit., p. 193.

disrupter. Temporary difficulty may arise when a people stands for the truth, but it is always compensated for by the peace which comes later. God has His own way of vindicating those who stand faithfully for the right. No blessedness was pronounced by Christ upon apostates, upon the religious leaders who opposed Him and His teaching—and such as now insist upon authority in the church-at-large. The true peace and purity of the church cannot be guarded too closely. This Beatitude strikes sharply at those contentious, stubborn, obstreperous church members who do not have the work of the Gospel and the glory of the Lord at heart.

It should be reiterated that the seventh Beatitude follows that which has to do with the pure in heart. James 3:17-18 is the commentary here: "But the wisdom that is from above is first pure, then peaceable, gentle, and easy to be entreated, full of mercy and good fruits, without partiality, and without hypocrisy. And the fruit of righteousness is sown in peace for them that make peace." The peace that is not based on truth is no peace at all. The pure in heart alone can offer to a lost and dying world-age that true peace which God will give to all who turn to Him in faith.

The Assurance in Which the Blessedness Consists

". . . Because just these shall be called sons of God."

hoti autoi huioi theou kleitheisontai

The emphatic pronoun autoi is used here for the last time, to stress the point which has been emphasized through the entire section, from verse 4 onward: only such as these described in this paragraph shall ever realize the blessedness here set forth. Only *these* shall be called "sons of God." The rendering of the Authorized Version is "children of God." The Greek word is huioi, "sons." The noun is used without an article to designate character, kind, and quality. Theirs is the *character of sons,* with the related standing and all the rights and privileges thereof. "Children" (tekna) carries the connotation of tender affection, and describes what we are by the new birth, whereas "sons" points to dignity and high standing. It indicates what God declares us to be by adoption (see: tekna, John 1:12; Rom. 8:16-17; huioi, Gal. 4:4-7).

It is indeed a high distinction accorded us to be called "sons of God" by God Himself, for the passive voice of the verb implies that it is He who assigns the title. No one else has the right and authority to do so. He alone can bestow the title in truth and reality. Again we find the future tense of the verb: kleitheisontai (from kaleo). It points to present as well as future time and refers to our being called "sons" even now, in accord with our business and work as peacemakers. Because Christ has "made peace by the blood of his cross" (Col. 1:20), God could manifest Himself as the "God of peace" (Heb. 13:20), and reveal Himself as "in Christ reconciling the world unto himself" (II Cor. 5:19-20). Thus we who have been reconciled to God are given the ministry of reconciliation, i.e., we are peacemakers, peace-diffusers. Hence God bestows upon us the title and distinction of "sons." For we are members of His royal family, with highest position in the Beloved One, and as such we carry to those who are not, the message of reconciliation. It is necessary that we reflect the image of our God as His dear children (tekna), and it is likewise essential that we possess the standing and dignity of "sons" (huioi), and thus in our peacemaking, be recognized for what we are: *God's own.*

Realization of the blessed assurance of sonship in our present experience is given by the Holy Spirit as He indwells us: "And because ye are sons, God hath sent forth the Spirit of his Son into your hearts, crying Abba, Father" (Gal. 4:6). The testimony of Romans 8:14-15 may be added: "For as many as are led by the Spirit of God, they are the sons of God. . . ." The full and complete manifestation of our sonship will, of course, come at the rapture of the saints in resurrection and translation, when we shall be brought into the very presence of Christ, and we are joined to Him in blessed spiritual union. This is known as the "redemption of [the] body" (Rom. 8:23; see also Eph. 1:14; I Thess. 4:13-18; Rev. 5:5-10, with I John 3:2), toward which we reach with groanings, yet look with anticipation, and to which we must be hastening, being diligent that we may be found by the Lord in peace, without spot and blameless, accounting that the longsuffering of the Lord is salvation.

As we close these remarks on the seventh Pronouncement, and approach the eighth, we note that the first seven Beatitudes have dealt with the saved, as to what they *are,* and should manifest themselves as *being,* in seven attitudes of character. The number seven indicates completeness. It is the number of the Lord Jesus Christ, the complete and perfect revelation of God. As we review this in our minds, meditating over these seven characteristics, applying them to ourselves, searching our own life and experience, we doubtless discover that we must bow our heads in shame and confession. *Not enough* of the image of our Lord is to be detected on our countenances, *not enough* of His character is seen in our attitude and behavior, *not enough* of the quality of His voice is heard in our speech. F. B. Meyer remarks, "The manners of the Heavenly Court are not evident enough in our demeanor," and Bishop Ryle writes:

> Let us learn how entirely contrary are the principles of Christ to the principles of the world. It is vain to deny it. They are almost diametrically opposed. The very characters which the Lord Jesus praises, the world despises. . . . Above all, let us learn how holy and spiritual-minded all believers should be. Sound doctrine is always the root and foundation, but holy living should always be its fruit. And if we would know what holy living is, let us often bethink ourselves who they are that Jesus calls *blessed.*[32]

---

[32]Op. cit., pp. 34-35.

8

THE EIGHTH PRONOUNCEMENT

"Blessed [are] they who are persecuted for righteousness' sake;
for theirs is the kingdom of heaven."

(v. 10)

Most expositors take this as the final Beatitude and include verses 11-12 under its heading, explaining that while "blessed" occurs twice, the second is evidently a repetition of the first, and that verse 11 is an amplification of the persecution set forth in verse 10. Thus we have a full and graphic description, with an emphatic and assuring conclusion.

We concur, in the main, with this explanation and agree that it is quite proper. Verses 10-12 are, without doubt, interrelated and to be taken together as referring to the same persecution theme. However in verse 11 there is a change of address to the second person plural, "ye" (the pronoun in the verb form). Moreover for the sake of clarity, and in order to simplify the outline and exposition, we shall divide at verse 11, and consider verses 11-12 by themselves as a ninth pronouncement, yet treating of the same general subject.

The Aspect of Blessedness

"Blessed [are] the ones persecuted for the sake of righteousness"

makarioi hoi dediogmenoi heneken dikaiosuneis

The reality of persecution

The objects of the persecution are indicated by the articular participle hoi dediogmenoi, which *"The ones persecuted,"* refers immediately to those who have been set before us and described in verses 3-9. All such are sure to become hated and persecuted. It cannot be otherwise in a world such as this. If we are actually in fellowship with the Lord, then of necessity, we shall be fellowshiping in His sufferings, reproach, and rejection. The servant is not better than his Master and Lord. We *know* that persecution must come. "If they have persecuted me, they will persecute you. . . ." This is definite and sure. Nothing is more certain. "Yea, and all that will live godly in Christ Jesus shall suffer persecution" (diochtheisontai, II Tim. 3:12).

The **character** of the persecution in the participle that is used. It is from dioko, used in the Greek writings frequently to designate "pursue," also in a lesser sense, "drive, chase away, drive a ship," or as a law term, "to prosecute." From it we finally get "persecute." In the New Testament, the word is used in a variety of ways, similar to its usages by Greek authors. It is used to express "flight, pursuit in a hostile manner, harassment, molestation, injury, driving someone away, endeavoring to acquire, keep pressing to reach a goal." However the central idea in the word, both in its classical and New Testament use, is a combination of "pursue" and "harass, treat evilly." These two ideas taken together aptly describe the character of the persecution suffered by the godly. Stier says,

> The essential idea of *persecute,* here, is to persist malevolently in seeking to withstand them; to transfer and carry on their enmity against God's righteousness, to its possessors and witnesses and ambassadors also. . . .[33]

We may call up the witness of the past, and refer to the terrible persecutions of Christians during the history of the church in all ages, particularly, perhaps, the Smyrna period, A.D. 100-300, when believers were pursued from place to place, hunted down like beasts, and put to death by the most inhuman, diabolical means. We today travel the path marked out

---

[33]Op. cit., p. 115.

by the tears and blood of these early martyrs, and it is an honor to do so. Never has the pressure of opposition and persecution ceased for the godly. Believers of this generation, living in this modern age and blessed as we are, for the most part, with the rights and privileges of freedom of worship in this part of the world, however, do not know persecution and have never known it as Christians of other ages and in other areas have known it. Yet the people of God have never been free from pursuit and persecution and are not now free from it. The enemies of the faith are many and they are powerful. They are constantly besetting us, ever in array against us, always seeking after us with intent to do harm.

Our enemies are men of this world-age, ungodly men who hate Christianity, though they themselves may assume great piety. Our enemies are the hosts of evil ones, the principalities, powers, and rulers of the darkness of this age, those whom we cannot see, under the leadership of the prince of the power of the air, Satan, the archenemy of God and of Christ. All of the evil forces of this world-order are arranged against the godly, and no time is lost when opportunity comes to do injury to the saints of God, even to bring about their death. In many parts of the world, men and women are imprisoned, exiled, and put to death for the Word of God and the testimony of Jesus Christ. Before the age ends with the return of the Lord in power and glory, many more will fall victim to the pursuit and hatred of the world's evil potentates and powers. But another Beatitude has been pronounced upon all who die for their faith: "Blessed are the dead which die in the Lord from henceforth. Yea, saith the Spirit, that they may rest from their labors, and their works do follow them" (Rev. 14:13).

The passive voice of the verb denotes the subject: the blessed ones, those whose character is set forth in the first seven Beatitudes, as receiving the action described by the participle. Commenting on this, Lenski notes that in all the previous pronouncements the designations indicate more than just inflictions; they show an inner attitude, and that such seems to be the case with the passive participle dediogmenoi. It is thus to be taken as permissive: these godly ones have allowed themselves to be persecuted and endured it willingly. They did not turn and flee from persecution when it came, but instead submitted to it. Whether the point is to be taken or not, we know of many faithful ones who have willingly and submissively borne the suffering when it came to them. They stood firm in grim trials and never recanted their convictions and confession of faith, but rested upon the great grace and mercy of God, trusting that they might not be ashamed and that Christ should be magnified in them "whether it be by life, or by death."

The participle dediogmenoi also indicates the **intensity** of the persecution. We take the perfect tense of the participle to be intensive, describing a past action, with emphasis placed upon the presently existing effects and results. When such emphasis is laid upon the results of an action, stress upon the existing facts is intensified. It is the strong way of saying that something *still is*. It sets forth the past event and lays sharp accent upon the resultant continuing state. So, here, we translate the perfect passive: "They who have been persecuted in the past and continue in that state." The thought is that persecution came to them in the past, and they keep on in the state of being persecuted ones because the persecution goes on. They have already been persecuted, and they will be persecuted again. There were trials and troubles before, and such will continue now. They held out, by the grace and mercy of God, under that persecution and continue in this state, some to the point of martyrdom. Those who have endured stood firm and true. The persecution of Christians that has raged in the past with such ferocity will not cease until this age is done. It will be present everywhere to some extent. Here and there it will break out with awful violence and viciousness. It will increase as the age draws to its close, but its greatest lasting effect is to bring out in bold relief the godly ones who endured it, who stood faithful and ture and held out under the abuse and oppression of ungodly forces. Our minds and hearts, fortified by a review of the past, with its testimony of faithful ones who have endured persecution (Heb. 11:1—12:2), must now be focused on the present, for we too—if we live godly—will suffer persecution, for "it is given in the behalf of Christ, not only to believe on him, but also to suffer for his sake" (Phil. 1:29). We are strengthened in our continuing state of persecuted ones, by the promise of comfort and mercy *now*. "If we suffer, we shall also reign with him" (II Tim. 2:12).

The Reason for Persecution: "On account of righteousness," heneken dikaiosuneis

As the first seven pronouncements set forth what the saved are by character, so here in the seventh Pronouncement, it is revealed what the manifestation of such character is sure to bring upon those who possess that character—persecution. And at once follows the precise statement as to the reason why persecution comes: "on account of righteousness." The Greek word for "righteousness," dikaiosuneis, is the same term as that used in verse 6, and it is used in the same sense, i.e., the integrity and purity of desire and life which inspires and dominates the believer's purpose and practice. Persecution comes upon Christians *because* of what they *are* in character and life. The Lord stated clearly, "If ye were of the world, the world would love its own; but because ye are not of the world, but I have chosen you out of the world, therefore the world hateth you" (John 15:19). The testimony of Christ in the believer provokes the resentment of the world's wickedness. The people of the world are not able to endure the rebuke of godliness. But let us be careful not to deliberately arouse the hatred and ill-feeling of others by what we do wrong, or by the manner in which we do what is right. *All* men will not hate us. *Some* will desire what is reflected in our life of godliness and exemplary conduct. However, let us walk circumspectly, not as fools, but as wise, because the days are evil.

Because of what the saved *are,* due to what God has made them by His grace, the world turns against them and persecutes them. They are obnoxious to the unregenerate masses because the very presence of the godly in their midst is a testimony against their own unrighteousness. The character of the godly as set forth here is particularly in the teeth of the spirit of the world. Poverty of spirit runs counter to the pride of the unbelieving heart. The repentant, contrite disposition which mourns over sin is not appreciated by the callous, indifferent, unsympathetic world. The meek and quiet spirit which takes wrong and is not quick to strike back is regarded as pusillanimous and rasps against the proud, militant, and resentful spirit of the world. That craving after deeper spiritual blessing from the Lord is a rebuke to the lust of the flesh, the lust of the eyes, and the pride of life, as is the merciful spirit to the hardness and cruelty of the world. Purity of heart contrasts sharply and painfully with hypocrisy and corruption. The peacemaker cannot easily be tolerated by the contentious, antagonistic world-age. It should be pointed out, however, that those who hate us and persecute us will not only be those who do not embrace any religion. They will be church members, those who belong to large denominational bodies or religious systems, who claim to be against us for the sake of God and because of the extremism of our faith. In certain respects, these are the worst haters and persecutors of all. The Lord said of such as these: "Yea, the time cometh, that whosoever killeth you will think that he doeth God service" (John 16:2). The astounding thing is not that true disciples will face death, but that their killers profess to be religious, even Christian. They think that such brutal murder is actually an act of offering service to God. Perversion of worship can go no farther than this, but it *will* go to this awful extremity.

Yet in spite of all this, irrespective of how men receive our witness, we must keep on in the midst of a crooked and perverse generation, among whom we must shine as lights in the world, holding to the Word of life. We must keep on being what the Lord wants us to be: "Ye have not chosen me, but I have chosen you, and ordained you, that ye should go and bring forth fruit, and that your fruit should remain. . . . And ye shall also bear witness. . . . In the world ye shall have tribulation: but be of good cheer; I have overcome the world" (John 15:16, 27; 16:33).

The Assurance in Which the Blessedness Consists

" . . . because theirs is the kingdom of heaven."

hoti auton estin hei basileia ton ouranon

In this course which we must travel, as the Lord's own, against the storm and opposition of a hostile world and its rulers, as we move on, enduring persecution, we have this blessed assurance: *ours is the kingdom of the heavens.* However men may treat us, whatever they may say or do to us, they cannot take away this blessedness, this grand possession. The Kingdom is ours by divine promise and grant. The wicked may set their mouths against the heavens and speak loftily. The ungodly may prosper and increase in goods and riches and seem never to be in trouble as others. They may plague the godly and with pride and arrogance say, "How doth God know?" Yet we must remember that the Kingdom of Heaven "is not out of this world-order." We do not look for it in this present scheme of things, for this is Satan's order. While we are now partakers and possessors in the reign of our Lord Jesus Christ over the earth, when He sits upon His throne of glory during the Messianic Era—it will be a vastly different order in which we shall rule. But the *fact,* and the *assurance* of the fact stand: "Theirs *is* the kingdom . . ." (see the exposition of v. 3).

9

THE NINTH PRONOUNCEMENT

"Blessed are ye, when men shall revile you, and persecute you, and shall say all manner of evil against you falsely, for my sake. Rejoice, and be exceedingly glad; for great is your reward in heaven; for so persecuted they the prophets who were before you."

(vv. 11-12)

The Aspect of Blessedness (v. 11)

"Blessed are ye when they shall revile you, and persecute [you] and say everything wicked against you by lying, for my sake."

markarioi este hotan oneidisosin humas kai dioxosin kai eiposin pan poneiron kath' humon pseudomenoi heneken emou.

The change to the second person, "ye," will be noted in this verse: makarioi este. The pronoun is found in the second person plural present indicative verb, este. Thus the present application of these Beatitudes is indicated, including particularly the last (v. 10). This present verb with its pronoun subject show how the disciples themselves are to apply this teaching, which includes the whole and not merely a part. We add Luke's "now." It is obvious that verse 11 is an expansion and description of the persecution noted in verse 10, but the applicatory second person also includes the rest. "Whenever," hotan, denotes any time when persecution takes place. Many instances of the mistreatment set forth here will occur. They are not to think it strange, nor are we, when it comes. We do not always know when it will come, for sometimes there is little or no warning. But whenever it does come upon us, we may know the reason for it and rejoice therein (see John 16:1-4; I Peter 4:12-14).

The persecution introduced in verse 10, and described in verse 11, is set forth in a threefold manner: (1) Persecution, in one's presence; (2) Persecution, by means of pursuit; (3) Persecution, against one's person.

The three verbs, oneidisosin ("revile"), dioxosin ("persecute"), and eiposin ("say"), are aorists, denoting definite and conclusive reality. We may be certain of this persecution, past, present, and future. The subjects are indefinite: "they." It is not necessary to make a specific reference, for all well know the significance of "they." It designates the enemies of Christ and His own, whoever, wherever they may be, all who oppose the message of the Gospel.

Persecution, in One's Presence

The third person plural aorist subjunctive verb oneidisosin is from oneididzo. In the Greek writings, as in the New Testament, the central idea of this verb is "to cast in one's teeth," as in Matthew 27:44. It is that reproach, upbraiding, and reviling that is done in our very presence—abuse that is cast at us, in our faces. Luke 6:22 has the same word, there rendered "reproach." True Christians know well what it means to be abused to one's face, with unkind and untrue words, with utterances that are vile and vicious.

Persecution, by Means of Pursuit

The aorist dioxosin, "pursue, persecute," is from dioko, which we have noted previously in connection with verse 10. It is the same word and designates pursuit with intent to do harm and injury, even to slay. (See the exposition of v. 10.)

Persecution, Against One's Person: "And say everything wicked against you by lying, for my sake." Kai eiposin pan poneiron kath' humon pseudomenoi heneken emou.

The verb eiposin, "say," denotes the decisive action of saying things, and pan poneiron ("everything wicked," or "every evil thing") marks the nature of the things said. Some texts have poneiron hreima, "every manner of evil words." poneiros, in the ethical sense, denotes that which is essentially evil and stresses the active exercise of the wicked disposition (kakia). It is the word used to describe Satan.[34] It designates evil things, vices that issue from the unregenerate inner nature (Mark 7:23).

In this passage, with kath' humon, which indicates the objects against which the speaking is directed, the word is employed to point out the vile and villainous slander directed against the godly. It emphasizes the evil nature of the things of which the saved are accused, the wicked, slanderous insinuations and accusations against those who belong to Christ—things affecting person and character. We are very careful about our character, anxious that it be unsullied, but if we live in close fellowship with the Lord, all manner of evil is certain to be imputed to us. Our motives will be impugned, our speech perverted, our actions misrepresented, and malicious tales circulated about us. The writer has experienced some of the worst of this. Ever since men called our Lord "Beelzebub" and took stones to stone Him, such vilification has befallen Christians. The present participle, pseudomenoi, is an adjunct of mode or manner and shows this form of persecution to be carried on by lying. Hence these wicked, slanderous sayings are utterly and deliberately false. The present tense stresses the continuing course of this form of persecution. It tells us that the world will never cease to hurl its vile epithets and lying accusations against those who know the Lord. But the middle voice of the participle points to those who engage in the persecuting. Theirs is a severe and solemn responsibility, for which they must one day answer to God.

Luke 6:22 includes the reproach (oneidisosin), but adds the ideas of hate (miseisosin): the hatred which stirs up and issues

---

[34]See poneiros in Matt. 5:37; 13:19, 38; John 17:15; Eph. 6:16; I John 2:13; 3:12.

in pursuit with intent to do harm, separation (aphorisosin): "mark off from others and exclude as disreputable"), and casting out one's name as evil (ekbalosin to onoma humon hos poneiron), which is similar to Matthew's thought of "saying all manner of evil against you by lying."

These are indeed painful inflictions and difficult to be endured. But our Lord added the words heneken emou, "on account of me," or, "for my sake." We bear these things on account of *Him,* for *His* sake. While this fact stirs our righteous indignation at the moment of enduring some evil attack, it soon causes us to realize that we must bear these things as *He* bore them: meekly, quietly, with no belligerent attempts at retaliation. Bearing this persecution on account of Him means bearing such persecution with the spirit in which He bore it. Slander will come, and difficult as it is to bear it, we do well not to attach too much importance to such censorious criticism launched against us. Abraham Lincoln once remarked that if he gave attention to all the criticisms that were directed at him, he would not have time for anything else. It is hard to accept the slanderous attacks that are made against us when we know that such charges are not true, but God knows what is said and who is saying it, and our vindication is in His hands.

Moreover we are sure that suffering for His sake is a righteous cause, for the Word leaves us no doubt. It is first said here that we are persecuted "for righteousness' sake" (v. 10a), and then that men shall persecute us "for my [Christ's] sake." Manifestly then, His cause is righteous, for He Himself is righteous. Righteousness is not an abstraction, for He embodies it. We suffer and bear persecution for a cause, that of truth, justice, righteousness, but it is more than merely a cause, for all of this is embodied in Him. Hence to suffer for the sake of righteousness is to suffer for His sake. To bear persecution on account of Him is to serve the cause of righteousness.

The Assurance in Which the Blessedness Consists (v. 12)

"Rejoice, and be exceedingly glad;
for your reward is great in the heavens;
for thus they did persecute the prophets before you."

chairete kai, agalliasthe hoti ho misthos humon polus en tois ouranois houtos gar edioxan tous propheitas tous pro humon.

The Attitude for the Persecuted: "Keep rejoicing and exulting,"
chairete kai agalliasthe

Two present imperatives are used to impress upon the disciples (also upon *us*) that state of mind and heart, and visible attitude, in which they *(we)* are to continue. Chairete is from chairo, "rejoice, be glad," and agalliasthe is from agalliadzo, "exult, rejoice exceedingly." Chairete by itself is not enough. Christ says, "Rejoice, but even more, exult!" (agalliasthe). They are to do this in full view of persecution, and under the pain and distress it will most certainly inflict when it comes—instead of falling into a state of lamenting, grieving, complaining, despairing, and as a result, failing to be what they should be. Never is this gladness and exulting to leave the godly. It is ever to be seen, no matter what they may be called upon to endure. The admonition is forceful because we generally lament and complain, and fall into despair, under the lightest tribulation. Yet to do so is to be disobedient in view of these imperatives. As Stier remarks:

> If ye are surely convinced in your heart and conscience that the reproaches of those who hate the righteousness of God, are falling upon you for *its* sake, then *rejoice and be exceedingly glad!* There is in this, as it were, a more emphatic command. . . .[35]

There is an outstanding example, found in Acts 5:17-42, of the manner in which the apostles themselves obeyed this injunc-

---

[35]Op. cit., p. 117.

tion. In this passage it is stated that they rejoiced (chairontes) "that they were counted worthy to suffer shame [and beatings] for his name" (vv. 40-41). It is also significant and of great interest to note how the Lord impresses upon His own the importance of their rejoicing and exulting in the face of persecution. This is indicated by the use of the middle voice of the verb, agalliasthe. *They* must be the ones who actually rejoice and exult, and *they themselves* are the ones who are mainly concerned in and affected by the results of their suffering and rejoicing over it. It is a responsibility of the Christian experience, and we cannot evade it.

The Adequacy of Their Recompense: "Because your reward is great in the heavens," hoti ho misthos humon polus en tois ouranois

The persecution comes with certainty and severity, and we are called upon to bear it, rejoicing and exulting in it. Now the adequate reason for rejoicing in such adverse circumstances is stated: "[Because] your reward is great in the heavens." The articular noun "reward," ho misthos, means "wages paid for work" (See I Tim. 5:8; James 5:4), but here not in the sense of anything earned by our works and sufferings, but in the secondary sense of "reward, divine recompense." God never permits that which is done for His glory to go unrewarded. Whatever is done for Christ's sake is rewarded with an abundance which comports with His greatness and glory and which is exceedingly far beyond our ability to conceive.[36] Polus, "great," describes the abundance, the greatness, of this reward.

36We do not serve the Lord for pay, and rewards for faithfulness and service are not the motivation for our labor for Him. We serve because we are called to do so, and because we love Him who first loved us, and called us. But the Lord, in His grace and His gentle condescension, has purposed to requite His own in His own incomparable way. Not only does the general reward of grace await us, but there will be for every affliction, every slanderous word we have to endure, for every reproach hurled at us, a distinct and divinely apportioned compensation. How good the Lord is!

This word is used in Revelation 7:9, of the uncountable multitude saved out of the great tribulation period; in Matthew 9:37,
of the great abundance of the harvest; and in Ephesians 2:4, of
the immeasurable vastness of God's love. Thus, the reward is
"great"—with a magnitude that is of God's own decree, hence
far exceeding any conception of reward known in the earthly
realm, not bestowed according to our merit, but according to
the grace, love, and mercy of the eternal God, our Saviour. The
Scriptures speak of crowns, and Peter writes of the inheritance
that is "incorruptible, and undefiled, and that fadeth not away,
reserved in heaven . . ." (I, 1:4). There is much which may
constitute this reward: the new body, the glories of heaven, the
release from the imperfect, corruptible things of this world-age,
the crowns—which are individual bestowments of reward.[37] But
perhaps the most wonderful of all is the blessed fact that we
shall be with Him who loved us and gave Himself for us.

Of this we are sure: the reward is "in the heavens." It is
treasure laid up for us *there,* where our Lord now is. It is not in
the earth, for we would not desire it there. Rather it is reserved
for us in the place where our names are written, where we hold
our citizenship, and where the great sovereign administrator of
the commonwealth of the saved is seated in the place of
authority and power. By assuring His disciples of their reward *in
heaven,* the Lord makes clear that His Kingdom is not of this
world that we prepare for it by witness-bearing against persecution here, and that it clearly attests the reality of heaven
itself. Where does this clear-cut testimony of Christ Himself to

---

[37]Nast states: "Here is something indicated that goes beyond the general
blessedness of the saints. The Lord who says that no cup of cold water
given to one of His disciples shall be forgotten, promises here graciously to
His followers a particular reward, a perfect indemnification for every
suffering which they have endured for His sake. Corresponding with your
sufferings shall be your reward. This, as well as other passages of Scripture,
plainly teach that there are different degrees of blessedness and glory in
heaven. The degree of our blessedness in heaven will be determined by the
extent of the capacity of blessedness which we have acquired here." Op.
cit., p. 248.

the literality and reality of heaven leave the skeptics who
disbelieve there is a real place called heaven—and the liberal
churchmen who teach their people that heaven is what one
makes of his earthly pilgrimage? They are put to shame by the
Lord's prayer to the Father: "Father, I will that they also,
whom thou hast given me, *be with me where I am, that they
may behold my glory* . . ." (John 17:24), and by Paul's testimony, "Henceforth there is laid up for me a crown of righteousness, which the Lord, the righteous judge, shall give me at that
day; and not to me only, but *unto all them also that love his
appearing*" (II Tim. 4:8).

The Attestation Concerning the Prophets

"For in the same manner they persecuted the prophets before you."

houtos gar edioxan tous propheitas tous pro humon

Here is the testimony of the past, which we may connect
with the perfect participle dediogmenoi in verse 10. "Blessed
[are] they who have been [in the past] persecuted for righteousness' sake [the persecution continuing]." It is as though
the Lord is at this moment reviewing those witnesses of the
truth of God who have suffered for it even from Abel's time. He
points to the prophets in illustration of this persecution in time
prior to the apostles. As Stier says,

> There is here graciously given to our weak faith another ground
> of joy in persecution, in that we perceive ourselves by this
> practical token to be companions of the prophets, the witnesses
> of God who have been before us; and thus become more and
> more assured of our citizenship in the kingdom of heaven, in
> contrast with the prevailing decay and destruction of all
> things.[38]

Houtos, "in this manner," indicates the manner in which the
prophets suffered. They were persecuted "in this way"—in the

---

[38]Op. cit., p. 118.

manner just pointed out as the varied, manifold way in which the Lord's disciples will be persecuted. They were reviled, slandered, assaulted; their names were thrown out as evil; they were pursued and slain. The prophets and the martyrs are placed on the same plane. The prophets stood and proclaimed God's truth, suffered for it, and died for it. Edioxan points to the fact that the prophets suffered this kind of persecution; it cannot be denied—there is the fact, definite and indisputable. In the same way the martyrs of Christ have witnessed for the Lord's glory and have been burned at the stake and butchered for it. But their testimony remains.

Their witness remains—for *us*. "Rejoice ye *in that day*" says Luke (6:23), i.e., in that day when you suffer persecution such as this, "for in the like manner did their fathers unto the prophets." *Their attestation is our inspiration.* By their testimony and witness we are urged and animated to endure. By their faithfulness we are impelled to lay aside every weight and the constantly besetting sin, and run with patience the race before us. Let us be willing to take up the cross and bear His reproach (Heb. 13:13), endeavoring to live godly and abide faithful as true Christians, continuing faithful in the doctrine of Christ, and ever walking in the truth. Blessed are all such! May the God of all grace grant that we shall not be ashamed or afraid to drink of the same cup which our Lord drank, confessing Him faithfully before men. He will confess us before the Father and the angels at the last day. "Great is your reward!"

Part Three

THE POSITION OF INFLUENCE IN THE WORLD OCCUPIED BY THE SAVED

(vv. 13-16)

The saved, described as to character in verses 3-9, will, by virtue of what they are and because of the One whose name they bear, be called upon to endure suffering and persecution during this present age. But they must learn to rejoice in that oppression and persecution for the sake of Christ, in view of their high calling and the certainty of their reward reserved for them in the heavens. And in consideration of the dignity and destiny of their calling, the less they must allow themselves to fall into any state of dispiritedness and doubt through the indignities and tribulations which will come, for they are actually *the salt of the earth and the light of the world.* Because of this they bear mighty influence, the extent of which can be known only by the eternal God Himself. The words of our Lord which follow in verses 13-16 insist upon and accentuate the indispensable continuance of active influence and faithful witness in the midst of an evil and antagonistic world-age. Stier writes:

> Ye—who have been described in vs. 3-10, who in your poverty have hungered for and have obtained righteousness, in order to the exercise of charity and peacemaking; Ye—who have been addressed in vs. 11-12, as having to expect, like the prophets before you, the ingratitude, scorn, and persecution of this world as your earthly reward, but an everlasting compensation for all

this, as your reward in heaven: *Ye are,* what grace has made you—*be*, and in joyful confidence continue to be, *all that your new nature requires!* Let no hindrance prevent this; look well to yourselves, that ye become not again incapable and unfit! First, altogether warning—woe to the savourless salt! Then again, though in part a promise—the light *must not* and shall not be hid! Finally, with fuller grace—then let the light which is given you, shine forth![1]

---

[1]Op. cit., pp. 118-119.

1

WE OCCUPY THE PLACE OF SALT

"Ye are the salt of the earth, but if the salt have lost its savor, with what shall it be salted? It is thereafter good for nothing, but to be cast out, and to be trodden under foot of men."

(v. 13)

The Designation Given

"Ye are the salt of the earth. . . ."

humeis este to halas teis geis

The Statement of Fact: "Ye are," humeis este

The pronoun "ye," humeis, is first in the sentence, thus bearing strong emphasis and having the force of "you, you alone—you only and no one else." This emphatic pronoun goes with the article in the predicate, to halas, "you *only* are *the* salt"—showing subject and predicate to be identical. We may as well say simply, "The salt of the earth is *you*." Humeis points to the disciples of Christ, but some attempt to limit it only to the apostles, or to pastors of churches. However the emphatic "you" does not carry that stress, and the passage itself discounts such an interpretation. All who possess the character which God bestows, and such as set forth in these pronouncements, are included in the plural "you." The pronoun includes all true believers, and emphasizes the great and blessed fact that *only they* are the salt of the earth.

The second person plural verb, este, states the fact, brings out

the reality. The saved *are* the salt. The stress here is on *being*—
what we really *are and continue to be.* Some see in this
statement an admonition as to what the saved *ought* to be, or
should *try* to be, or what God *wants* them to be. But the fact is
stronger than that: humeis este shows what believers *are,* and as
Lenski remarks, "If they are not salt, then they are not believers." The present tense of the verb (este, from eimi) denotes
the continuing course of those who are the salt. Ours is the
character of salt *now.* It is not a case of our *getting to be* salt,
but the incontrovertible fact is stressed that we *are* salt now,
and *continue to be* salt. The present, continuing reality is made
plainer to us, and still more strongly impressed upon us, by the
warning which follows. Let us remember then, that *we are* the
salt of the earth.

The Significance of the Salt: "The salt of the earth," to halas
teis geis

The article "the," to, goes with the pronoun "you," humeis, as
already pointed out. It seems quite clear that "salt," halas, is to
be taken in the sense of that which arrests corruption. While it
is true that salt is used to protect food from putrefaction and to
preserve it and make it palatable, the figure taken in its context,
in the light of the description of the character of those who are
the salt, sets forth the power that opposes and counteracts
corruption.[2] The point is that the holy, Christlike living of the
saved, in consistency with their character, will serve to oppose
and arrest the moral corruption of the inhabitants of the earth
(teis geis).

---

[2]Nast states: "The property of salt is to season that which is insipid, and
to preserve that which is corruptible. Exactly corresponding to these
physical effects of salt, or ought to be, the moral influence exerted upon
the world by the followers of Christ." But the tasty seasoning effect of the
salt *does not imply* that we must make concessions to apostate religion,
and accommodate our message of truth to the secular mind of the
world-age. This made crystal clear by the following statement in v. 13, "if
the salt have lost its savor, with what shall it [the earth] be salted?"

Our presence in the earth as true Christian believers, among the multitudes of the earth-dwellers, acts as salt to check the rottenness in which the world is perishing. Stier says,

Salt alone averts corruption, and gives a good and savoury taste (Job 6:6), hence it appears in the sacrifices as the seasoning, and a sign of the covenant of God. Without salt the earth is corrupt before God (Gen. 6:11), and all who live upon it foul and stinking, an abomination in His sight" (Ps. 14:3).[3]

It is quite likely that most of us have not stopped to consider this carefully. *We are the salt of the earth.* Our presence here, then, is a rebuke to, and a censure of, worldliness and the sensuality of the people of the world. Our presence here will arrest, to some extent, the commission of crimes. It should silence certain kinds of conversation and check the flow of improper and ungodly words when we enter the room. Because of our presence many kinds of worldly amusements which have become a part of numerous professedly Christian home and family habits, should be felt out of place. Our presence should turn men's thoughts toward God, at least for a few moments, and should command a certain respect on the part of some. Our presence must immediately condemn untruth, oppose apostasy, and put the lie to incorrect and erroneous theological teaching. Right through the society in which we live and move and have our being, there should be an awareness of something about us *unlike the rest,* a consciousness that there is an incongruity between our character and conduct, and all that savors of impurity, falsehood, insincerity, and selfishness. Besser remarks, "The world would prefer that we were honey instead of salt."

The Scope of the Salt's Influence: "the earth," teis geis

We are the salt *of the earth.* The articular genitive teis geis is as appropriate for "earth," as tou kosmou is for the following

---

[3]Op. cit., pp. 119-120.

figure of light. It designates the masses of earthly people upon whom the salt is to work. It adds the distinct note of universality and thus carries far beyond Palestine and the localities of the early church. This thought that we are the salt of the earth—the entire earth—is vast and tremendous indeed, above the ability of our human minds to fully comprehend. It startles and humbles us. But the Lord knows the condition of the earth—that it is like a carcass slowly but surely deteriorating, disintegrating, and rotting to putrefaction, in dire need of some powerful influence to stay the corruption. This was so when He Himself came into the world. It was the state of things when His disciples went everywhere preaching the Word, and it is most assuredly so in our day. With all our modern inventions, modes, and appliances, with all our advances in science and culture, with all present-day organization, education, religion, and our boasted civilization, the decay goes on and the corruption continues. The masses of human society are affected to some extent, in an external manner, by modern culture and civilization, with their philosophy, humanitarianism, and ideas of social betterment. Yet the fact remains that if it were not for the presence of the true church of our Lord Jesus Christ and the witness borne by the words and lives of her members, the salt and light influence of the saved, there would be nothing to save the world from its corruption and final destruction. So—we are the salt *of the earth*. Everywhere Christians are salt and must make their presence known and felt as salt. *We only are the salt.* If corruption is stayed, it is through our presence in the earth that God will do it. Hence the warning follows.

The Danger Indicated

"... But if the salt have lost its savor, with what shall it be salted? It is thereafter good for nothing, but to be cast out, and to be trodden under foot of men."

ean de to halas morantheien tini alistheisetai; eis ouden ischuei
eti ei mei bleithen exo katapateisthai hupo ton anthropon

Illustrated by a Representative Case: "But if the salt have lost its savor, with what shall it be salted?" ean de to halas moranthei en tini alistheistai

"If," ean, introduces a hypothetical condition, described by to halas moranthei en tini alistheisetai. Moranthei the aorist passive subjunctive from moraino, "make flat and tasteless," used of salt that has lost its strength and flavor (see the passage in Luke 14:34). The aorist designates the fact and stresses the reality of the loss, "if [as the case supposes], the salt has actually lost its strength and flavor...." En tini alistheisetai expresses the logical question in view of the opening statement, "With what shall it be salted?"—i.e., by what means shall it receive again its salting power?

Some make much of the fact that Jesus Christ would not use a figure that is taken from something which does not actually occur in nature. But the Lord *did* use such figures. What person would light a lamp and then deliberately set it under a bushel? Certainly, these "impossible" figures emphasize and bring out most vividly the reality which the Lord teaches. Lenski remarks,

> Let us acknowledge the fact that Jesus used such figures with a mastery that goes beyond all "good writers." The very idea of salt losing its saltiness! But that is what may happen in the case of Christians....[4]

Still, any debate with regard·to whether or not salt may really become insipid and lose its taste is not relevant here, for Christ *sets down the case*. And the point of the case lies in the supposition that if the salt does lose its savor, the consequence will be as here described. There is no suggestion as to the possibility of believers falling from grace and losing their salvation. The question is not, Can Christians ever lose their position in Christ, and thus become disinherited from eternal life which they once possessed? The issue is not, If believers lose their

---

[4]Op. cit., p. 200.

faith, how shall it be restored to them? Rather, If Christians lose their salty savor, by what means will they again receive it? *This* is the point. So what then *is* the issue of Christians who lose their salty flavor and strength, and who are thus found wanting in that quality which can stay the corruption of the world and season the tastelessness of an all-pervading carnality?

Impressed upon Us by the Solution to the Case: "It is thereafter good for nothing, but to be cast out, and to be trodden under foot of men." Eis ouden ischuei eti en mei bleithen exo katapateisthai hupo ton anthropon

The matter of whether or not Christians fall from the place of saving faith, and whether or not they are restored, has no place here. The issue is not one of salvation, or of the security or nonsecurity of the believer, but of *service*. Eis ouden ischuei clearly sets forth the utter uselessness of the salt for the purpose for which it was designed—not exclusion from the community, not excommunication from the church, not the loss of salvation. The description is that of the unfitness and uselessness of those whose influence and testimony are intended to act as salt in staying corruption, but whose witness has become savorless. The injunction is that such are fit for nothing any longer except to be thrown out and trampled under men's feet. The bleithen exo katapateisthai hupo ton anthropon clause is an expression of rebuke and contempt.

Thus the purpose of this figure is clear. It denotes service, not salvation; diligence and devotion, not departure from the faith. A view of the calamitous effects which would follow disobedience, negligence, and disregard of this warning is used by the Lord as a means of preserving from such catastrophe and preventing it. You who are true believers, described as to character in verses 3-10 and addressed in verses 10-12 as having to expect, like the prophets before you, the ingratitude, scorn, and persecution of the world, nevertheless must be all that your new nature requires. You must bear your active influence and testimony in the midst of an evil world-age. You are the salt of the earth, let nothing prevent your living and acting as salt. Perform your function. Take heed to your doctrine and to your conduct. Look well to yourselves, that you do not become inactive, unfit, savorless; because salt that has lost its savor is useless. If you become useless, then you must be disapproved and discarded; you will become castaways (I Cor. 9:24-27).

2

WE OCCUPY THE PLACE OF LIGHT

"Ye are the light of the world. A city that is set on a hill cannot be hidden. Neither do men light a lamp and put it under a bushel, but on a lampstand, and it giveth light unto all that are in the house. Let your light so shine before men, that they may see your good works, and glorify your Father, who is in heaven."

(vv. 14-16)

The Designation of the Light

"Ye are the light of the world."

humeis este to phos tou kosmou

The Significance of the Light

The sentence begins with the same statement of fact as that in verse 13, "Ye are," humeis este, The emphatic pronoun is placed together with the present tense verb, to show that the disciples of Christ alone, *only they,* are the light of the world (see the exposition of v. 13). The definite article "the," to, goes with the emphatic pronoun humeis as in the case of to halas. As salt is for corruption, so light is for darkness. The function of the light is here said to be that of *shining* (v. 16). "And the light shineth in the darkness . . ." (John 1:5a). As the salt counteracts the corruption in the earth, so the light shines with the truth in a world of ignorance and untruth. As the salt is to oppose and check the foulness in the earth, so the light is to oppose and reveal the falseness in the world. True believers in

Christ are *the light,* to phos, having been lighted with the light
of life in Christ (John 8:12). We are *the light,* having been called
out of darkness, and we must now walk as children of light
(Eph. 5:8). We ourselves are the light, just as the Lord says, but
we shine with light that emanates from a center, and He who is
Himself within us is that center. Our shining radiates from Him.
David said, "The Lord is my light . . ." (Heb. "my *shining,*" Ps.
27:1).

"The light," to phos, is the light of good works, i.e., the
works of faith, thus ordered in the Word of God, under the
ministry of the Holy Spirit. It is the light of the character of
Christ Himself revealed in His own. It is the light of living as He
lived, the light of fellowship—constant fellowship—with Him. It
is the light of the life of truth, love, faithfulness, and consistency, which opposes untruth, reveals sham and pretense, and
exposes the lie. It is the light of devotion to the Lord, dedica-
tion to our calling, and diligent obedience to the Word of God.
It is the light of a daily godly life; it is performing and fulfilling
the Lord's instructions in these pronouncements. It is *being* the
light of the world, as He said. We shine by what we *are.* We
shine because our shining comes from Him who bought us and
made us His own. We shine as more of the radiance of Christ
and less of the wick of our own nature and disposition is seen.
We *are* the light, yet we have no light of our own. It is
important for us to note that the Lord does not say that we
must wish ourselves to shine. He does not say, "Shine ye," but
rather, the peremptory aorist imperative: "let *your light* shine!"
True—we *are* the light, but our light is *derived, bestowed,* so
that *we have* the light: "he that followeth me shall not walk in
darkness, but shall *have* the light of life" (John 8:12). We need
this aorist command, lampsato, "Shine! Do it! Let that light
definitely shine!" The works of faith must genuinely radiate
from the light of Christ within us. Lenski's comment is most
fitting:

> In our day of humanitarian works and "charity" and a "moral
> life" without Christ, the chief works by which the faith of

Christ's disciples shines out and must shine out deserve special attention: the acts of true Christian worship, the support of Gospel teaching and preaching at home and afar, the stand against error and all anti-Christian and unchristian religious forces, the fearless confession of the divine truth, the loyalty to the principles of this truth under all circumstances, the readiness to bear ridicule, slander, loss, and persecution of all kinds for the sake of the faith and the truth of the Word.[5]

The Scope of the Light's Influence

We are the light "of the world," tou kosmou, this present order, structure, and arrangement of things; the aggregate of all things earthly; the whole circle of earthly institutions and goods, with the endowments, riches, adornments, advantages, pleasures, ways, and means, etc., including the inhabitants of the order; the whole mass of unregenerate men and women, alienated from God, and thus hostile to the cause of Christ.

This is the world in which we must let our light shine; a world existing in spiritual darkness, a whole order of things which lies in the dominance and power of the archenemy of God—Satan, the prince of this age. But it is a world of *men,* human beings like ourselves, who need the redemption which the Son of God wrought, in order that men might believe in Him, and thus not perish but have everlasting life. Hence it is before *men* that our light must shine—those men of this very age into which God has put us as the light. His purpose for us is that we let our light shine before men so that they may see our good works (ta kala erga). We cannot force them to believe, but they must see these good works in order that, if possible, they may be brought to the place of glorifying our Father who is in the heavens.

---

[5]Op. cit., p. 203.

The Description of the Light

The Example of the City (v. 14b)

"A city that is set on a hill cannot be hidden," ou dunatai polis krubeinai epano orous keimenei

The point here is the conspicuousness of the city which is set on a mountain top. Everyone can see it, and—if need be—find refuge there. Its light will be seen for many miles around. So it is with *us.* Our light will make us *conspicuous.* We are like the city—we cannot be hidden. We are not members of a secret organization, like the pagan mysteries, and the various lodges, cults, and secret orders of our day. Rather, we are *the light,* the spiritual light, meant for conspicuous shining in this age of darkness. As such we are likened to the city on top of the high hill, which everybody can see. Stier says,

> The light of the pure word and of holy life is to burn brightly and loftily for the dark world, which also itself is, and shall be made a House of God. No human ordinance, no false shame or fear, may place this light under a bushel, which is designed to shine forth from word and work combined.[6]

And Marcus Dods suggests that:

> Christians are not to retire and hide themselves, satisfied if they can keep their own souls alive. They are to enter into all the innocent relationships and engagements of life, and so use them as to show their light. . . . If your conduct is to teach a better way to men, your conduct must be seen. It is of the essence of Christian character to shine, to become visible. . . ."[7]

The Example of the Lamp (v. 15)

Neither do men light a lamp (KJV, "candle"), *and put it under a bushel, but on a lampstand, and it giveth light unto all*

6Op. cit., p. 123.

7*Pulpit Commentary, Gospel of Matthew* (New York: Funk & Wagnalls Co., 1944), 1:204.

that are in the house." Oude kaiousin luchnon kai titheasin
auton hupo ton modion all epi tein luchnian kai lampei pasin
tois en tei oikia.

This is a second illustration to emphasize the fact that light is
meant to be conspicuous, and that it is intended for somebody's
help. The plural verbs kaiousin and titheasin negatived by oude,
are indefinite, with their subjects in the verb forms—"they . . .
they," denoting *they, anyone.* Neither does anyone light a
lamp, or a candle, and then set it under a peck-measure, but
they place it on the lampstand, where it belongs, and there it
shines for all those who are in the house. The idea is clear:
nobody lights a lamp and then hides it under a cover, but puts it
where it is meant to be, in the place made for it, on the
lampstand where it may shine and be seen and give light for all
that are in the house. It may be that a Christian may, for some
reason, think to hide his light (though God forbid!), hence this
second illustration is given. Christ has not lighted us to be
placed under cover and be hidden from sight. We have been
lighted *to shine,* to occupy that place where we can act as lamps
to all in the house.

The Exercise of the Reality (v. 16)

*"Let your light so shine before men, that they may see
your good works, and glorify your Father, who is in heaven."*

houtos lampsato to phos humon emprosthen ton anthropon
hopos dosin humon ta kala erga kai doxasosin ton patera
humon ton en tois ouranois.

The Manner of the Shining

How the light is to shine is indicated by "so," houtos, "in
this manner." Our light is to shine constantly in the manner set
forth in the context, by the illustrations given, in the manner by
which a city on a hill cannot be hidden, in the manner by which
men light lamps and put them on the lampstand, where they

shine and give light to all in the house, instead of placing them under a cover which conceals the light. Hence, in the manner of *a true light* we must shine—conspicuous, bright, illuminating, penetrating, and giving off benefit to all.

The Responsibility of the Shining

"Let your light shine," houtos lampsato to phos humon. The aorist verb lampsato (from lampo, "shine, give light") points out the definite and complete reality of the shining. It is *"Let your light shine. . . ."* The light with which we have been lighted is indeed *real.* It *does shine* and will *keep* shining with blessed and decided reality if we do not cover it. Hence it is our prime and binding responsibility to *let this light shine.* It is not we who ignite the flame, nor do we supply the oil, but we are charged with carefully guarding against anything coming in which may obstruct, or cover over the shining of the light. The imperative lampsato intensifies the reality and urgency of the matter: "You *must* let your light shine!" This stresses the fact that it is our *duty*—our sacred duty and office—to stand guard firmly and faithfully against all that might hinder the telling effect of our testimony and influence. It underscores the solemnity of our responsibility. Let each one of us earnestly desire and pray to our Father, that it shall be said of us as was said by the Lord of John the Baptist: "He was a burning and a shining light!" (John 5:35).

The Objects of the Shining

The phrase, *"In the presence of men,"* emprosthem ton anthropon, indicates the objects of the shining.

We are to see to it that our light goes on shining before the people of the world, among whom we walk day after day. The definite article with the noun "men" points particularly to the unregenerate: *"the* men, the men of the world system, those men who are unsaved." It may have an even more specific reference to those who persecute and revile us. For, as Stier remarks, "This is to be our only retaliation"—our faithful shining. Whatever our station in life, wherever our place in this world, God has chosen it and appointed us to do it, and it is that particular place where we can—and must—do our best work. *There* we must shine, in the presence of men.

The Purpose of Shining

The phrase, *"that they may see your good works,"* hopos idosin humon ta kala erga, clearly indicates the aim of shining.

Hopos, "that," designates *purpose:* the light must decisively shine before men, *in order that*—or, *to the end that*—"they may see your good works." The testimony of our good works is for men to behold and from which they are to draw much good. The record of James, which stresses the priceless value and the inestimable need of a life of good works on the part of believers, thus stands forth as all-important. These works are the works for which believers have been newly created in Christ, the works which God has prepared beforehand that we should walk in them. They are works only for those who have been saved by grace through faith. In these days of humanitarianism and churchianity, of religion without Christ and the Gospel, of world-wide departure from the faith of historic Christianity, it is imperative that we walk as children of light and that we keep uncompromisingly to the path of truth and godliness.

We may draw a contrast between these good works (the character of which has already been set forth in verses 3-10 and developed somewhat from verse 20 onward), and the works (religious externalities of self-righteous religionists) set down in 6:1-2. "Let your light so shine before men, that they may see your good works . . ." and "Take heed that ye do not your alms before men, to be seen of them . . ." appear superficially to be conflicting statements. But this is not the case. The Lord would not say one thing and then contradict His pronouncement with a different statement. Rather, in this way, the true is distinguished from the false; the works of faith are made distinct from the works of religious externalism. According to Ephesians

5:8-14, the walk of the children of light does not, cannot, conceal their revealing, witnessing light-nature. And the bright shining of the saved exposes the falsity and the unfruitfulness of the works of darkness and makes manifest their evil character.

The Motive of the Shining

The phrase, "and glorify your Father, who is in the heavens," kai doxasosin ton patera humon ton en tois ouranois, indicates the impelling motive for letting one's light shine.

That men should behold the shining of our excellent works is indeed the immediate aim of our letting the light shine, but the motive supreme is this: that you may glorify your Father who is in the heavens." The psalmist wrote, "Not unto us, O Lord, not unto us, but unto thy name give glory . . ." (115:1). We can have no higher motive than this, can be impelled by no other desire than this. Then we serve God effectively and acceptably. I *must let my light shine:* I must guard with my life against anything that would oppose and cut off that shining, for it must shine—it *will* shine—for my Heavenly Father's praise and glory. These good works of faith, as we are led into them through the Word ministered to us by the Holy Spirit, shine with a heavenly brightness in this world of darkness and sinful works. The light will draw some to saving faith and help others to shine more brightly. Bishop Ryle's words are indeed appropriate:

> Surely, if words mean anything, we are meant to learn from these two figures, the salt and the light, that there must be something marked, distinct, and peculiar about our character, if we are true Christians. It will never do to idle through life, thinking and living like others, if we mean to be owned by Christ as His people. Have we grace? Then it must be *seen.* Have we the Spirit? Then there must be *fruit.* Have we any saving religion? Then there must be a difference of habits, tastes, and turn of mind, between us and those who think only of the world. It is perfectly clear that true Christianity is something other than being baptized and going to church. *Salt* and *light* evidently imply *peculiarity* both of heart

and life, of faith and practice. We must dare to be singular and
unlike the world. . . .[8]

It is not by mere coincidence that the Lord returns to the
mention of something at the close of the paragraph (v. 16) to
which He has referred three times previously (vv. 3, 10, 12).
The reality and literality of heaven have become controversial in
our day, as has also the question of whether God is a real
person, an idea, a concept of human reason, or the product of a
highly imaginative interpretation of Bible passages which speak
of Him. But the words of Christ settle the matter beyond all
doubt, all question. Our light must shine as the Lord intended
so that men might see it, and through it get to know the Lord
and thus glorify *our Father who is in the heavens.* Heaven, then,
must be a real, literal place, and God must be a real person. Else
how is it that our Father can be there?

The appearance of the definite article in the last clause of
verse 16 is of interest and significance, ton patera humon ton en
tois ouranois, literally, "The Father of you, the One in the
heavens." Three times the definite article is used in this brief
clause. *"The* Father of you" denotes the person of God the
Father of all who are His true children, as distinct from any and
all other so-called fathers. The second article, placed after the
pronoun "of you" ("your," humon), identifies *"the* Father" as
the very One whose place of habitation is "in *the* heavens"—
described by the words en tois ouranois. Tois, "the," is a part of
the title, sometimes rendered in the plural, occasionally in the
singular, descriptive of heaven. Yet the article also serves to
distinguish *heaven* from *earth,* identifies it *as a place,* and
discounts it as a mere figment of the imagination or a human
philosophical idea.

Hence the Lord, while emphasizing the present propriety of
these great pronouncements and impressing upon us the need
for such traits of character and conduct *now,* as we maintain
our walk and witness in the face of opposition and persecution,

---

[8]Op. cit., pp. 36-37.

He at the same time fortifies us, establishes us, and strengthens us with these words of blessed assurance regarding the certain and absolute reality of those two great essentials of the Christian faith: the actuality of God our Father as a real Person, whose children we are by faith, and the literality of His abiding place in heaven, where our family-home is in readiness.

Father, grant us the grace so needful to enable us to occupy our place in this world as salt, and as light, during these days of corruption and darkness, of moral disintegration and apostasy, and keep us faithful in that place, guarding with our very lives against all that would cause the salt to lose its savor, and against all that would hinder and cut off the shining of the light—to the eternal praise, honor, and glory of Him, whose we are, whom we love, and whom we serve—in the name of Christ, Amen!

ADDITIONAL NOTES

PART TWO

Chapter 1

Despite Gill's comment in Broadus' Commentary on Matthew, that ptochoi ("poor") in the first pronouncement should not be pressed to mean "beggars," we insist on the sense of "beggarly poor ones" as the legitimate rendering of the Greek word. It does not at all suggest the inappropriate notion that believers go about "begging." The term describes Christians with reference to their inherent state, not to a physical condition of life, nor does it imply a future reception of reward and gifts. Our poverty of spirit stands in contrast to self-sufficiency, and our consciousness of insufficiency makes us dependent upon Christ. In this we are "blessed."

Chapter 2

It has been pointed out by certain writers that Christ does not specifically define that which causes the mourning in the second pronouncement, and does not name the mourning as the result of sin. However, while it is undeniably true that the earthly life is full of physical sorrow, suffering, and pain, the connection of the text points definitely to *spiritual* mourning. The poverty of the first pronouncement is that of the spirit, so then is the mourning of the second pronouncement. As the deepest poverty lies in the realm of the spirit, so the deepest mourning lies there also. The poverty of the beggarly poor in spirit leads to mourning over sin, unworthiness, and the slowness of our spiritual progress. As Williams remarks, "All other mourning is but partial and slight compared with this." Consider Proverbs 18:14: "The spirit of a man will sustain his infirmity; but a wounded spirit, who can bear?"

Chapter 3

The "meekness" of the third pronouncement is not easy to define precisely, and has been misunderstood and misinterpreted. While we have dealt adequately with the term praoteis in the discussion of the third pronouncement, these additional comments are not inappropriate. The word certainly involves freedom from pretension (I Peter 3:3, 15), and a patient endurance of ill-treatment and injury—when it is proper to endure. Williams suggests that the thought here is primarily "that of meekness exhibited towards men (as seems evident from the implied contrast in the clause "they shall inherit the earth"), yet meekness towards men is closely connected with, and is the result of, meekness towards God." Here, meekness might be defined as the attitude of the soul towards another when that other person is in a state of activity towards it—the attitude of the pupil to the teacher when teaching, the attitude of the son to the father when exercising his parental authority, the attitude of a youth to an older and wiser man when advising in a vital matter. Hence it is essentially as applicable to the relation of man to God as to that of man to man.

Trench says: "The Scriptural praoteis is not in a man's outward behavior only; nor yet in his relations to his fellow-men; as little in his mere natural disposition. Rather it is an in-wrought grace of the soul; and the exercises of it are first and chiefly towards God. It is that temper of spirit in which we accept His dealings with us as good, and therefore without disputing or resisting."

Chapter 4

The figure of hungering and thirsting for spiritual things is not infrequent in the Old Testament Scriptures, e.g., Isaiah 55:1, "Ho, every one that thirsteth, come to the waters, and he that hath no money; come, buy and eat; yea, come, buy wine and milk without money and without price." The thought in the fourth pronouncement has been debated: Is it the *craving* or the actual *participation* which is preeminent? The text requires the craving as central here. The consciously poor in spirit mourn over their sinfulness and spiritual poverty and long for that personal godliness and righteousness that habitually does what is right, good, and holy. It does not mean that we shall be filled now once and for all, so that we shall never again have desire for more. We become filled, but then we need to be filled again and again, and our hunger and thirst grow so that we need more and more. We have no righteousness of our own, so we need *His*. The true Christian longing is for righteousness *first*, and this includes godliness, holiness, purity—then happiness and peace follow. "The work of righteousness shall be peace; and the effect of righteousness, quietness and assurance forever" (Isa. 32:17).

The accusative noun tein dikaiosunein ("righteousness"), has a special interest in view of the fact that in the Greek writings the verbs peinao ("hunger"), and dipsao ("thirst"), are frequently followed by the genitive case. But here the noun is in the accusative and carries the definite article. The craving is for *the whole lot*—not just a part of it. And it is the only righteousness worthy of the name. It is for *this* righteousness and all that it includes for which the believer longs, and longs again, because the desire for it bespeaks the sense of sin and weakness, and therefore the need for it.

Chapter 5

Our blessed Lord stresses an element in the mercy of His fifth pronouncement, which most of us do not recognize in the quality of mercy. We generally think of mercy as not dealing severely with another, not inflicting punishment when it is due, or sparing a fellow-human some great pain, or particular hardship, or labor. But the unusual quality of this mercy (eleeos) is the active kindness shown to one in trouble. It is love and compassion showing themselves in action and reaching out to those who are in need. Those who show mercy in this way to others, shall themselves be the recipients of mercy in their own time of need.

Chapter 6

The Pharisees were indeed scrupulous about legal purity, bodily purification, and the Levitical distinctions between the clean and the unclean. Our Lord Jesus Christ insists upon purity *of heart*—which cannot be limited to the absence of unchaste feelings and impressions, but also to freedom from all the defiling influences of sin upon the inner man. As Broadus remarks: "We must shun defiling thoughts, purposes, and feelings." James says: "Purify your hearts, ye double-minded" (4:8).

To eat with unwashed hands is a violation of social etiquette, but it does not defile us as the legalistic religionists said it did. But evil thoughts, murders, adulteries, fornications, unlawful desires, physical lusts, sensual cravings, thefts, blasphemies, etc., whether only conceived in thought or carried out in deed—these defile us. The heart that is pure has no hidden motives, selfish aims, underlying a fair and honest external appearance. Moreover, the pure in heart "shall see God." They see Him now by faith, and as Williams remarks: "Purity of heart cleanses the mental vision; the pure in heart see mysteries of grace, of love, and of holiness, which are hidden from the eyes of the unclean. He manifests Himself to those who keep His Word. And in a more glorious vision, 'we shall see Him as He is. And every one that hath this hope in him purifieth himself, even as He is pure' " (I John 3:2-3). See Psalm 24:3-4 on the whole thought.

Chapter 7

Broadus says: "It is not easy to be a peacemaker." Much is required of a peacemaker. He must have tact, courage, wisdom, skill, knowledge of human nature, love. The age in which we live is characterized by envy, jealousy, ill will, hatred, diverse rivalries, party spirit of various kinds in every community, so many feuds dividing men from men—all of which make it most difficult to realize the blessedness of this beatitude.

Still, it is not intended that the Christian shut himself away from the world in a monastic seclusion, indifferent to the evils of the age around him. There are times when he must interfere for good. It is a dangerous process, and most apt to be misunderstood because the peacemaker is often held to be an enemy of both sides of a quarrel. But the peacemaker's greatest work is the making of peace between God and men through the preaching of the blood of the cross (Col. 1:20). We are blessed in the practice of this pronouncement, but we attain it only as we let the peace of Christ rule in our hearts (Col. 3:15; John 14:27).

Chapter 8

Bishop Ryle states: "The Lord Jesus calls those blessed who are perse-cuted for righteousness' sake. He means those who are laughed at, mocked, despised, and ill-used, because they endeavor to live as true Christians." Simply stated, this is precisely the point in the Lord's statement. Broadus adds: "The expression obviously points forward to the persecution of His followers, but it is well to remember that at the probable time of His delivering this discourse, Jesus Himself was already beginning to be bitterly hated and reviled, and His life sought." It should also be said that even the prophets before Him had suffered persecution because of their message. His disciples were presently not among the hoi dediogmenoi ("the ones being persecuted"), but were in all probability experiencing the beginnings of the reproach and reviling referred to by the Lord. They would feel the surge of the world's hatred because of Christ and would in time be baptized with the baptism with which He was baptized. For *us* today the offense of the cross remains. There is persecution still, and it will continue and increase. True godliness is not popular for it is a rebuke to this world-age and its people.

PART THREE

Chapter 1

The idea that the salt (to halas) is for *seasoning*, and the view that its purpose is that of *fertilizing*, are not at all in harmony with the text. That Christians are merely to keep life from becoming stale and flat, and nonproductive, is the view propagated by many liberal theologians. Salt does its work as a preserver, a preventive, a purifier. The presence of Christians in the world is intended for the accomplishment of the same work. Salt is *antiseptic*—we are expected to be of the same character, not merely to be pure, but to purify. We are not here *to get* good, but to impart that which is good. Our calling is to counterwork the corruption of this age. Ryle remarks: "Salt has a peculiar taste of its own, utterly unlike anything else. When mingled with other substances it preserves them from corruption. It imparts a portion of its taste to everything it is mixed with. It is useful so long as it preserves its savor, but no longer. Are we true Christians? Then behold here our place and its duties."

The world into which our Lord Jesus Christ was born, the one in which His disciples later served and bore witness of Him, was a materialistic-minded, vice-laden world, corrupt and evil despite its opportunities, glamor, opulence, genius, and grandeur. But the infusion by a comparative few of a new way of life, a new life of purity and godliness into the mass of society could not then and cannot now be denied. It is impossible to correctly calculate the influence and advantage to this world-age of the presence in it of the body of true believers. As Robert Tuck has aptly commented: "Both salt and light are silently working and interior-working forces. Neither makes a loud noise. The one works away at the arresting of corrupting processes, the other works away at the quickening and invigorating of life, but neither has any boasting to make. You must put salt *into* things and hide it *in* them. And the light cannot do its full work until it gets *inside* things. Its surface-work is its least work." So it is with our Christian witness. We must get it *inside, within* men's hearts, where it will bear fruit. So it must be given in its full truth, with accuracy and authority, and with conviction in its power.

Chapter 2

The first clause of verse 16 has a particular significance because of the position of the words in the Greek sentence: houtos lampsato to phos humon. There is a special emphasis upon "so" and "shine," which are the first two words in the statement: "in this manner shine," e.g., "in this manner let your light shine." The first word in the sentence, "so" (literally "in this manner"), refers specifically to the way signified by the image in the preceding statement in verse 15. Our light of personal witness—which consists in the good word of the Gospel and the good works of the godly life—is to shine so as to be *seen* and *received*.

BIBLIOGRAPHY

Alford, Henry. *The Greek Testament,* vol. 1, "Gospel of Matthew." London: Rivingtons, Waterloo Place, 1863.

Barnes, Albert. *Notes, Explanatory and Practical, on the Gospels,* vol. 1, "Gospel of Matthew." New York: Harper and Bros., Publishers, 1853.

Bloomfield, S. T. *The Greek Testament, with English Notes,* vol. 1, "The Gospel According to Matthew." Philadelphia: Clark and Hesser, 1854.

Broadus, John A. *An American Commentary on the New Testament,* vol. 1, "Gospel of Matthew." Philadelphia: The American Baptist Publication Society, 1886.

Bruce, A. B. *The Expositor's Greek Testament,* vol. 1, "The Synoptic Gospels, Gospel of Matthew." Grand Rapids: Wm. B. Eerdmans Publishing Co., n.d.

Caffin, B. C. *The Pulpit Commentary,* vol. 1, "Gospel of Matthew." New York: Funk & Wagnalls Co., 1944.

Cramer, Raymond L. *The Psychology of Jesus and Mental Health.* Los Angeles: Cowman Publications, Inc., 1959.

Geldenhuys, Nowal. *Commentary on the Gospel of Luke.* Grand Rapids: Wm. B. Eerdmans Publishing Co., 1956.

Jacobus, Melancthon W. *Notes on the Gospels, Critical and Explanatory,* "Matthew and Mark." New York: Robert Carter and Bros., Publishers, 1873.

Jamieson, Robert; Fausset, A. R.; and Brown, David. *A Commentary, Critical and Explanatory on the Old and New Testaments,* vol. 2, "Gospel of Matthew." Hartford: The S. S. Scranton Co., n.d.

Lange, John Peter. *Commentary on the Holy Scriptures,* "The Gospel of Matthew." Grand Rapids: Zondervan Publishing House, n.d.

Lenski, R. C. H. *The Interpretation of St. Matthew's Gospel.* Columbus: The Wartburg Press, 1943.

―――― *The Interpretation of St. Luke's Gospel.* Columbus: The Lutheran Book Concern, 1934.

MacDonald, J. A. The Pulpit Commentary, vol. 1, "Gospel of Matthew." New York: Funk & Wagnalls Co., 1944.

Meyer, H. A. W. *Commentary on the New Testament,* vol. 1, "Gospel of Matthew." New York: Funk & Wagnalls Co., 1884.

Nast, William. *A Commentary on the Gospels of Matthew and Mark.* New York: Carlton and Lanahan, 1870.

Ryle, J. C. *Expository Thoughts on the Gospels,* vol. 1. Grand Rapids: Zondervan Publishing House, 1951; Reprint, 1956.

Smith, David. *Commentary on the Four Gospels,* vol. 1, "Matthew." New York: Doubleday, Doran & Co., Inc., 1928.

Stier, Rudolph. *The Words of the Lord Jesus,* vol. 1. Philadelphia: Smith, English and Co., 1855.

Vincent, Marvin R. *Word Studies in the New Testament,* vol. 1, "The Gospel According to Matthew." Grand Rapids: Wm. B. Eerdmans Publishing Co., 1946.

Williams, A. L. *The Pulpit Commentary,* vol. 1, "Gospel of Matthew." New York: Funk & Wagnalls Co., 1944.

Zodhiates, Spiros. *Poverty, A Blessing or a Curse?* New York: American Mission to Greeks, Inc., n.d.

―――― *Persecution.* New York: American Mission to Greeks, Inc., n.d.

―――― *Slander.* Ridgefield: American Mission to Greeks, Inc., n.d.

―――― *Meekness.* Ridgefield: American Mission to Greeks, Inc., n.d.

LEXICONS AND EXEGETICAL SOURCES

Arndt, Wm. F., and Gringrich, F. Wilbur. *A Greek-English Lexicon of the New Testament.* Chicago: The University of Chicago Press, 1957.

Cremer, Hermann. *Biblico-Theological Lexicon of New Testament Greek.* Edinburgh: T. & T. Clark, 1954.

Deissman, Adolph. *Light From the Ancient East.* Grand Rapids: Baker Book House, 1965.

Harkavy, A. *Hebrew-Chaldee Dictionary.* No frontispiece.

Lambert, J. C. *The International Standard Bible Encyclopedia,* vol. 1, "The Beatitudes." Grand Rapids: Wm. B. Eerdmans Publishing Co., 1939.

Scott, Robert, and Liddell, Henry George. *Greek-English Lexicon.* New York: Harper and Bros., 1870.

Moulton, Jas. Hope, and Milligan, George. *The Vocabulary of the Greek Testament.* Grand Rapids: Wm. B. Eerdmans Publishing Co., 1960.

Pickering, John. *A Comprehensive Lexicon of the Greek Language.* Philadelphia: J. B. Lippincott Co., 1889.

Robinson, Edward. *A Greek and English Lexicon of the New Testament.* London: Longman, Orme, Brown, Green, and Longmans, 1837.

Thayer, Joseph Henry. *A Greek-English Lexicon of the New Testament,* rev. ed. New York: The American Book Company, 1889.